UNDERSCORE

By

FRANK SKINNER

The timing sheets reproduced herein are printed with the permission of Universal Pictures Company, Inc., the copyright owner of the photoplay for which the music in this book was written.

MT
40
.S 75
1960

THE MECHANICS OF FILM SCORING
(35mm Film)

(A) Film is projected at 90 feet per minute.

(B) There are 16 frames of picture in one foot of film.

(C) One foot of film equals two-thirds of a second.

The following table shows a breakdown of one minute with the footage and the seconds.

FILM FOOTAGE TABLE
(In Seconds)

FEET	SECONDS	FEET	SECONDS	FEET	SECONDS
1	⅔"	31	20⅔"	61	40⅔"
2	1⅓"	32	21⅓"	62	41⅓"
3	2 "	33	22 "	63	42 "
4	2⅔"	34	22⅔"	64	42⅔"
5	3⅓"	35	23⅓"	65	43⅓"
6	4 "	36	24 "	66	44 "
7	4⅔"	37	24⅔"	67	44⅔"
8	5⅓"	38	25⅓"	68	45⅓"
9	6 "	39	26 "	69	46 "
10	6⅔"	40	26⅔"	70	46⅔"
11	7⅓"	41	27⅓"	71	47⅓"
12	8 "	42	28 "	72	48 "
13	8⅔"	43	28⅔"	73	48⅔"
14	9⅓"	44	29⅓"	74	49⅓"
15	10 "	45	30 "	75	50 "
16	10⅔"	46	30⅔"	76	50⅔"
17	11⅓"	47	31⅓"	77	51⅓"
18	12 "	48	32 "	78	52 "
19	12⅔"	49	32⅔"	79	52⅔"
20	13⅓"	50	33⅓"	80	53⅓"
21	14 "	51	34 "	81	54 "
22	14⅔"	52	34⅔"	82	54⅔"
23	15⅓"	53	35⅓"	83	55⅓"
24	16 "	54	36. "	84	56 "
25	16⅔"	55	36⅔"	85	56⅔"
26	17⅓"	56	37⅓"	86	57⅓"
27	18 "	57	38 "	87	58 "
28	18⅔"	58	38⅔"	88	58⅔"
29	19⅓"	59	39⅓"	89	59⅓"
30	20 "	60	40 "	90	1.0"

To continue, you add ⅔ of a second for each foot of film.

THE USE OF A CLICK TRACK
(A tempo guide—heard through earphones)

(1) To catch intricate cues on the screen by writing accents to fall on the corresponding clicks, which will hit the cues automatically. (See pages 94, 95 and 96 of "Underscore.")

(2) To speed up, or make recording easier, if the music is to be in a steady tempo. This eliminates any variation of tempo by the conductor. It also makes the ending of the cue automatic.

(3) To record the correct tempo to dancing, such as a cafe scene which has been shot to a temporary tempo track to be replaced later. The cutter makes the click track from the original tempo track.

(4) To lead into a rhythmic piece of music already recorded. The click track is made in the correct tempo and the number of bars can be adjusted to fit.

(5) To insert an interlude betwen two pieces of music, if rhythmic, to fit perfectly in the correct tempo.

(6) To record any scene that has many cues and is difficult for the conductor. The music does not have to be all rhythmic to require the use of a click track. The composer can write in a rubato manner to the steady tempo of clicks.

MAKING A CLICK TRACK
PROCEDURE: *(with tape)*

(1) The composer determines a tempo. For example: eight clicks (or 4 bars of two-four, or 2 bars of four-four music) in 3 seconds.

(2) The music cutter, or editor, punches holes in a strip of *blank leader* so many frames apart, which when transferred to tape by the sound department, produces a clicking sound (When the leader is run on a machine, the light passing through the punches produces the sound.)

(3) There are two types of tracks: a loop—which is a short strip spliced together—or a continuous track for the length of the scene. Loops are adequate for a dance tempo, but for a scene with cues to hit, a continuous track is used.

(4) The cutter determines how many frames apart the clicks should be for a certain tempo by a mathmetical formula.

FORMULA:

(a) There are 24 frames of picture in one second.

(b) There are 4 sprocket holes in one frame.

(c) A track for 8 clicks in 3 seconds is figured by multiplying the number of frames (24) by the number of seconds (3), then divide by the number of clicks (8). For example: $24 \times 3 = 72$ divided by 8. The answer is 9, or a nine-zero (9.0) track.

Nine-Zero means that the clicks are nine frames apart. When the answer is 10.5—or 10½—the clicks are ten frames and two sprocket holes apart, the two being one-half of the four sprocket holes in a frame.

TABLE OF TEMPO TRACKS

CLICKS SECONDS	TYPE	CLICKS SECONDS	TYPE
8 clicks in 3 ”	9.0	8 clicks in 5 ”	15.0
8 clicks in 3⅓”	10.0	8 clicks in 5⅓”	16.0
8 clicks in 3½”	10.2	8 clicks in 5½”	16.2
8 clicks in 3⅔”	11.0	8 clicks in 5⅔”	17.0
8 clicks in 4 ”	12.0	8 clicks in 6 ”	18.0
8 clicks in 4⅓”	13.0	8 clicks in 6⅓”	19.0
8 clicks in 4½”	13.2	8 clicks in 6½”	19.2
8 clicks in 4⅔”	14.0	8 clicks in 6⅔”	20.0

It is possible to make a variable track to catch action not in strict tempo. For example: a man walking. He may vary so the cutter can make a track to fit his steps.

(Note: Before tape, a click track was made by scraping the emulsion off the film to let the light pass through to create the click sound.)

TAPE

35mm TAPE—is used for theatrical films. One tape can carry 3 channels, or more, (called stripes by soundmen), controlled with separate dials on the dubbing panel. (Elaborate stereo is sometimes done on more than three channels—possibly seven.)

(a)   One channel—orchestra (not stereo).

(b)   Two channels—possibly a vocal and orchestra.

(c)   Three channels (stereo)—different sections of the orchestra on separate channels.

ONE QUARTER INCH TAPE—is used for commercial records and transferred to disks. The speed is—15 inches a second.

For home recording, etc.—speeds of 7½, 3¾ and 1⅞ inches a second. Speeds less than 7½ are not good for music.

16mm FILM

16mm FILM—is projected at 36 feet per minute with 40 frames of picture per foot. A dubbed 35mm picture can be transferred to 16mm film.

(Before tape, all recording and dubbing was done with film.)

TECHNICALITIES

WILD TRACKS—For background music, such as radio, cafe, etc., recorded "wild"—(not to picture).

(a) Recorded longer in length than the scene.

(b) The cutter syncs from the beginning (the introduction, or the start of a chorus) with no ending—the mixer dials it out.

(c) Dialed in—to let it enter in the middle of a phrase, to give the effect that the orchestra has been playing, and is still playing as the scene finishes. (Dialed out—no beginning or ending.)

(d) Separate recording of a cymbal crash—a tympany note, or roll,—celeste or piano chords—vibraphone chords, or bells, etc.—which the cutter sets up in sync.

WARNING CLICKS—are sometimes added ahead of a vocal (before the tape is transferred to an acetate for playback) to warn the singer when to start singing with the pre-recorded playback.

Clicks added to a long note to warn the singer when to cut off. This also helps the side line orchestra because they will be using the orchestration that was pre-recorded and just go through the motions of playing.

Warning clicks are not necessary if the number is rhythmic and has a definite introduction.

DANCE ROUTINES—The same procedure is followed (with warning clicks, if not rhythmic) as with a vocal. (Every number should be pre-recorded.)

CAFE, OR BALLROOM DANCING—A selected tempo track from the library is used for shooting and the music recorded for it later—unless the orchestra is prominent—then the results are better if the music is pre-recorded, and the same orchestration used in the scene, so that the right instruments are playing at the right time, especially the violins bowing correctly.

(The timing and the writing of dramatic underscoring is explained in "UNDERSCORE.")

CONTENTS

CHAPTER ONE

PREPARATION

THE TECHNIQUE of scoring a picture can be applied to one made for the theatre, or one made for television. Pictures being mechanical, it is necessary that the music be written to a set footage, which is transferred into seconds and becomes measured music, by employing a stop-watch, in order to fit into the confines of a certain length of film. (As the book progresses you will see how this is done with actual timing sheets, with the action and dialogue timed to the split second.)

Due to the mechanical problem, the only way the music can be written to fit the film, is to wait until the picture is completed and edited in its final cut in order to write the music. If you wrote a scene at random and they cut five feet of film out, or added five feet, the music would not fit. The only time this problem arises is when they preview a picture and are forced to make certain cuts. If the music cannot be cut in some manner to make sense, a second recording session may be called to re-record the cut scenes, after the music has been reconstructed.

The first thing to be done when the picture is edited, is to sit in on a general running of the picture. This running is just to absorb its content. Next, the picture has to be broken down, reel by reel, to decide which scenes require music. Each scene is discussed, generally with the Producer and Director to determine where to start and stop the music on these scenes.

Each reel is numbered and each scene is lettered. For instance, the main title at the beginning of reel (1) is called (1A,) the next scene is (1B,) etc. A film for television may only be in three reels, whereby a theatrical film may be ten reels, or more.

1

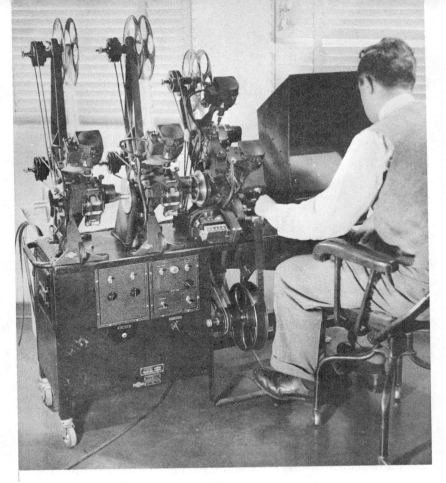

A Moviola . . .
Used by Film Editor and Music Cutter

After breaking down the film, the music cutter will retire to his cutting room and break down each scene on a moviola, (see picture) which has a footage counter and a small viewing screen. This machine can be started, stopped, or reversed with a foot pedal. The music cutter will describe the action and dialogue to a stenographer, who in turn makes up the typewritten notes. The cutter starts to time at zero, and when important action or dialogue happens, he can stop the machine, get the reading on the footage counter, and tell at what split second it happens. When he has completed the timing sheets, it reads like a script, only the timing readings are indicated. It is possible at this stage to write the score without looking at the picture again.

2

CUE LINES AND DUBBING

When writing the score. the composer plans to accentuate certain dramatic impacts. or a change of mood on certain cuts of the picture. These important cues are indicated with a line, or streamer, which starts at one side of the film and runs diagonally across to opposite side. When it reaches the opposite side, that is the conductor's cue. When recording, the conductor follows a stop clock on the podium, watches the timing on his music, and catches the cues with the aid of the cue lines. When you study the timing sheets and sketches that follow, you will notice that the cues (circled on timing sheets) are indicated with a double line on the sketches. which will be marked with a streamer on the film for recording.

Dubbing is the final recording of all the elements of sound. such as music. dialogue and sound effects, from separate reels of film onto one soundtrack. All of these tracks are placed on separate machines. called dummies. and they are piped into a large panel of dials. operated by several men into a final composite recording. (see picture of machines on page 124).

First. the music is transferred from tape. on which it was recorded. to film. so separate reels can be constructed in sync, for the scenes for which it was written. If one cue segues to another. the second cue must be on a separate reel to overlap, so the mixer can dial out the first cue and dial in the second. Therefore, the music must be written so this can be done, such as, relative chords, etc., (you will see examples in the score to follow).

Another problem confronting the composer, is a reel change-over, when the operator changes from one machine to another. For example, if we have a scene with the music playing to the end of reel (1) and continues into reel (2), the same technique is used, such as relative chords or a sustained note. (see examples in the score).

CHAPTER TWO

WRITING A SCORE

ONE OF THE main differences between television and motion picture scoring is the size of the orchestra employed.

Motion Pictures are made on a more elaborate scale, therefore a large orchestra is usually used. Writing for a smaller orchestra is somewhat more difficult, and the music has to be composed very carefully to be effective with a small group of instruments. After one masters the technique and develops a feeling for creating musical moods, it should be more simple to write the type of material for the orchestra at hand.

TYPES OF SCORING

There are two types of scoring, namely: pre-scoring and post-scoring. Pre-scoring means that the music is recorded prior to the shooting of a picture, such as songs, dance routines, and any musical numbers that have to be photographed.

Post-scoring means that the music is recorded after the picture is shot, such as a dramatic or comedy picture, where the music has to fit the action. A song is pre-recorded on the recording stage, then played on the shooting stage with a playback machine and photographed while the singer mouths the lyric in sync. Dance routines are shot the same way, the dancers dance to the playback machine while the picture is being shot silent. Later, when the cutter lines up the music tracks with the picture, it seems that the singer, or dancers, are performing with the orchestra. If the singers are recorded on a separate track from the orchestra, either element, singer or orchestra, can be replaced if not satisfactory. Also, each track, voice or orchestra

4

can be controlled in the dubbing. This procedure can be done by either pre-recording the orchestra first and then have the singer use earphones and record the voice alone, or it can be done with an isolation booth for the singer, with both the singer and conductor using earphones.

DANCE ROUTINES

Sometimes a dance routine is shot with a temporary track, such as a piano alone, or a small group of instruments, which is replaced later with a new orchestra track. On rare occasions, a song may be sung live on the shooting stage while the scene is being shot, however this is not satisfactory, because the sound is not up to par and limits the cutting, or editing.

CLICK TRACK

When writing a score, sometimes a scene presents itself where the precision should be so near perfect that the human element would make it almost impossible to record. Such a scene is a comedy routine where the composer would like to catch every little gag on the screen. This is made simple by using a click track. The cutter can build one by scraping a thin line in the emulsion of the film, so many frames apart, depending on the desired tempo. When this is piped to the conductor's earphones he hears the click of the tempo. The composer tells the cutter the tempo he wishes, for example, four bars of two-four music in four seconds. The cutter makes the click track two clicks to the bar and gives a detailed breakdown of the scene in clicks, rather than seconds. The composer can then write effects to fit the action on certain clicks; for instance, a man gets hit on the head on click three, an accent in the music on the downbeat of bar two will help this comedy. The action can also be caught in between clicks, such as click $3\frac{1}{2}$, if so, the accent would be on the second eighth note of bar two.

Remember, there are two clicks to a bar of two-four music. With the conductor following the clicks in his earphones, the music falls into place automatically.

TELEVISION

When writing a score for television pictures, the composer will find a few problems not found in theatrical films, namely: commercials. The length of a TV film is planned to insert a commercial at the beginning and at the end, everything stops in the middle also, for another commercial. In other words, the show is in two acts instead of a continuous show. Therefore, short musical endings must be composed to end Act One. These are short, but should come to a definite end. Also, in a TV picture, a device is employed to tie in one scene into another, which is called a bridge. These bridges should be in the mood of the outgoing scene. If dramatic, the music should describe this mood and tie into the mood of the following scene. The same applies to a comedy. The music can help the comedy if humorous music bridges these scenes.

Sometimes the narrator describes the action, this may happen at the end of one scene and the narrator describes the following scene to a certain point. Then, the picture goes to live dialogue. This type of writing would be in a manner such as this, to end the outgoing scene with some dramatic chords, or a phrase, if the picture is dramatic. Then continue the music softly, under narration, ending the music when the dialogue goes live.

MOODS

There are several schools of thought about scoring a picture. One is strictly mood music with no thematic relation to the characters in the story, another, with thematic and melodic writing.

Some pictures, especially TV detective stories with City locales, lend themselves to a jazz treatment, pizzacato bass and cymbal provide a mysterious background to construct menacing jazz phrases, building to wild sounds for a fight, or dramatic punch.

I prefer thematic and melodic writing for most pictures, for two reasons. It is more understandable to the layman, and it conveys more emotion than a series of chords. I realize that a melodic line will detract the viewers' mind from the picture at times, if the melody attracts their attention, but in a tender scene, or one of sorrow, a melodic line will enhance and convey the real emotion of the actors.

I also realize, it is better writing to play for mood at times in a dramatic scene, one long dramatic chord says more here than any melody can do. In fact, a melodic line could possibly hurt the scene.

In the following pages, we will study a score that I wrote for a picture which we will call "THE IRISHMAN." We will study the timing sheets, sketches and actual orchestrations. (Technical explanations will appear in italics.)

Although this score was written for a large orchestra, the technique would be the same as if written for a smaller orchestra. The only difference is you would not get involved by using a smaller amount of instruments.

First, we will discuss the different types of themes and see how I planned the themes for "THE IRISHMAN," after reading the script.

There are many types of love stories, such as sincere love, which has a little tear and sorrow behind it, a light, gay

romance; a teen-age puppy love, which is sweet; a sophisticated love; and a very intense, dramatic love.

For example, a theme for a sincere love scene, with a
feeling of sadness, could be . . .

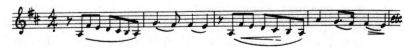

This theme has a certain amount of pleading and anxiety in
its character.

A theme for a light, gay romance could be . . .

This theme can be transformed into a gay waltz . . .

A theme for a teen-age puppy-love could be:

This is simple in character, and not too serious.

A sophisticated theme could be:

The chord construction of this theme gives it a feeling
of sophistication and offers opportunities for rhythmic patterns, such as . . .

A theme for an intense dramatic love scene could be . . .

This has strength, emotion and sincerity.

A story generally consists of three elements: Love, menace, and comedy.

Menace can be described in many different ways. You can describe menace with only one note . . .

Or with different types of chords . . .

Or with a melodic line or a phrase . . .

A menace theme is more effective in the lower register and should be one that can be developed into greater length. The phrase (A) could be developed . . .

Although the first bar identifies the theme, it gives you possibilities to develop. This complete phrase could remain - in the bass with an interesting upper-line . . .

Or alternated in the upper-voices . . .

The phrase (B) could be developed . . .

The phrase (C) could be developed into a canon . . .

Comedy themes are of the opposite character and could be a phrase that has odd intervals . . .

Themes. most generally. identify the different characters in a story. and sometimes are referred to as "so-and-so's" theme. This does not mean that you have to use "so-and-so's" theme every time he or she appears — in its original straight form — or use it at all if some neutral mood music would be better — but these themes give you material to develop into the mood of the scene.

For the score of "THE IRISHMAN". it was possible to develop the main themes of the picture before the picture was finished shooting and edited, by studying the script. The themes for the less important characters would develop as the score was being written. Here is the story in brief:

THE STORY

O'TOOLE, a swashbuckling wanderer, inherits his family home. an old castle. He comes back to Ireland to claim it. On his way he rescues a lady, (MAUREEN) whom some thugs are trying to kidnap. She is traveling by carriage, to her father's home in Dublin. Her father. an Englishman, holds a high office in the diplomatic service. Her fiance. (LORD STANHOPE) is also in the service. but is really conspiring with the French, represented by (HENDRIGG). to attack England through Ireland.

O'TOOLE organizes a group which foils the plot and exposes the traitors. winning the lady's hand. (A girl, KITTY, and two thugs, JACK and PAT. assist in the kidnapping plot).

There are four main characters: O'TOOLE, as the leading character; MAUREEN. the love interest: HENDRIGG, STANHOPE and KITTY. the menace.

In the opening scenes. after the main title, you will find O'Toole walking across the countryside toward home. The plotters are waiting for Maureen's carriage to pass, but O'Toole upsets their plans.

Naturally, you will be able to identify the themes, developed on the following pages, for certain characters. The principal theme should be Irish in character and one that can be used in different forms. It should be gay and carefree in one form and then noble and sincere in another.

After a period of time I made a lead sheet of the following theme:

— PRINCIPAL THEME —

I then made a lead sheet of the tune in another form:

I then decided to add another line to that, so I wrote:

The new line in itself was of Irish character and was a tune that could be played alone. One was counterpoint to the other. It would depend on the orchestration which line would predominate.

The secondary theme had to be of a light, romantic character. The love scenes in this script were of a light variety, and consequently the theme had to be written accordingly. I finally wrote the following lead sheet:

– LOVE THEME –

Next came the menace theme, and after giving it some thought I made a lead sheet of the following:

– MENACE THEME –

I decided to add to this something that I could use in different places to put more emphasis on the menace so I continued:

This could be used with horns and trombones or tympani and be very effective.

The comedy in this script was a girl character, rather dumb, so after some deliberation I wrote:

– COMEDY THEME –

This could be used in both the upper and lower registers.

There were also two old Irish characters in the script who were played for comedy, but I thought it would be better to wait until the picture was finished before writing any material for them.

There was a secondary love story running through the

script involving English characters who were associated with the heroine's father in the diplomatic service. It was of a rather serious nature so I wrote a theme that was the opposite of the Irish one—sympathetic and sincere:

To this I added a bass line:

This, I thought, would orchestrate well and be exceptionally fine for strings and wood-winds.

There was another character in the story who intrigued me. She was a French countess whom O'Toole had met in his wanderings, and she went to Ireland to see him. She flitted in and out of the picture and presented an opportunity for something cute, musically speaking. I decided a string pizzicato movement would fit her, but also that it should have a French flavor. I wrote a short theme to be developed later:

This had a saucy flavor and seemed to fit her.

When I wrote this score, I examined the timing sheet for the main title, which read:

                    MUSIC I-A   MAIN TITLE
   0.00   Start to fade in on "TRADEMARK."
   0.02⅔   Fade full in.
   0.07⅓   Start to fade out.
   (0.10)   Fade full out—Start to fade in on Super Pictures
             presents "THE IRISHMAN."
   0.12⅔   Fade full in.
   (0.19⅓)   Middle of diss.—To "WITH CARD."
   0.26   Middle of diss.—To "AND CARD."
   0.36⅔   Middle of diss.— To "SCREENPLAY CARD."
   0.42⅔   Middle of diss.—To "PHOTOGRAPHY CARD."
   0.48   Middle of diss.—To "ART DIRECTOR."
   0.54⅔   Middle of diss.—To "SONGS BY."
   1.02⅔   Middle of diss.—To "COSTUMES BY."
   1.07⅓   Middle of diss.—To "MUSIC BY."
   1.12⅔   Middle of diss.—To "PRODUCER."
   1.18   Middle of diss.—To "DIRECTOR."
   1.22   Start to fade out.
   (1.24⅔)   Fade full out.

The reason for the thirds of a second is that film runs through a projection machine at the rate of one foot per ⅔ of a second.

The film cutter or editor cuts by footage, therefore the cuts most generally time in fractions of a second.

After planning which cues I would catch, I decided to catch only two at the beginning; the fade-in on the "SUPER PICTURES PRESENTS" card and the dissolve to the "WITH" card. I would have a smoother composition by not trying to catch the others.

It was a custom for years to build up to a climax with fanfares and cymbals on the producer and director cards, but it is considered on the "hammy" side today.

The first cue would be at ten seconds and the second at nineteen and one-third seconds (as circled on the timing sheet.)

A Film Splicing Machine

I planned to open the picture with a broad statement of the Love or Secondary theme over the Trademark. At ten seconds I would change to a bright treatment of the principal theme over the "PRESENTS 'THE IRISHMAN'" card; it would be carefree and full of life. At nineteen and one-third seconds I would change into the broad version of the same melody; this would continue up to one minute, twenty-four and two-thirds seconds or the fade-out.

Main title music should always set the mood of the picture to follow. Generally I write the title last because there is

*a greater selection of material in the score so that it will be
more representative.*

As I started the sketch , it looked like this:

*In analyzing the sketches you will see that the orchestra
was kept in mind during the writing. This has two advant-
ages: (1) The composer has the orchestra at his command to
create moods by planning an instrumentation color in advance,
and (2) It restrains you from writing too pianistically. (Many
compositions written for piano are not practical for orchestration.)*

*The orchestra instruments have definite tone-color and
convey different moods. For instance:*

*A FLUTE can be gay in the upper register, but lone-
some and rather cold in the lower register.*

*The OBOE, pastorale, gay and sweet, while the ENGLISH
HORN has a rather sad and mournful sound.*

*The FRENCH HORN is noble and sincere in the middle
and upper registers, but ominous in the lower register.*

*The VIOLIN is sweet and sympathetic. The VIOLA, with
its rather nasal tone, is not as warm as the violin.*

*The CELLO is very warm and sympathetic. As a whole,
the string section creates warmth and sympathy, and also
dramatic tension and suspense if played tremolo.*

*With this in mind, the composer can indicate to the ar-
ranger what instrumentation he thinks is best for the scene. A
good arranger will study a timing sheet in advance to select the
best instrumentation for a scene even though it may not be
indicated.*

*Analyzing the sketch for the main title, we find the sec-
ondary theme in the strings, the wood-wind with a pastorale
pattern, and the brass with an organ effect. This section is
over the Trademark.*

*At ten seconds when the "presents" card starts to fade in,
it changes to the principal theme in a gay mood, played by the
full orchestra and with a change of key.*

*At nineteen and one-third (0.19⅓) seconds it changes to
the noble treatment of the same melody with a change of key.
At bar twelve (12), a ritard is planned to broaden the tempo
in the next section. Here the contrapuntal treatment is used
with the French horns playing the principal theme, reinforced
with a trumpet. The violins play the upper line.*

Notice the timing markings throughout the number above

A Playback Machine

the staffs. A desired tempo must be planned in advance as well as the correct number of bars of music. The timing is noted on the conductor's sketch to enable him to know just where he is when recording in relation to a stop clock or watch.

Compare the following orchestration with the preceding sketch.

MAIN TITLE

I-A

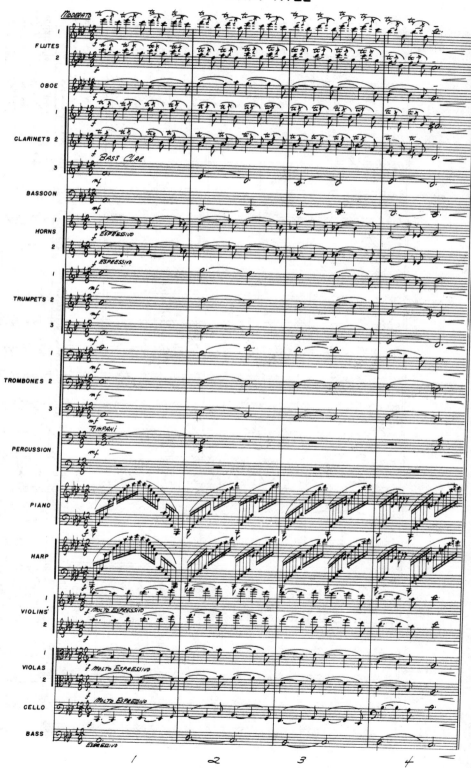

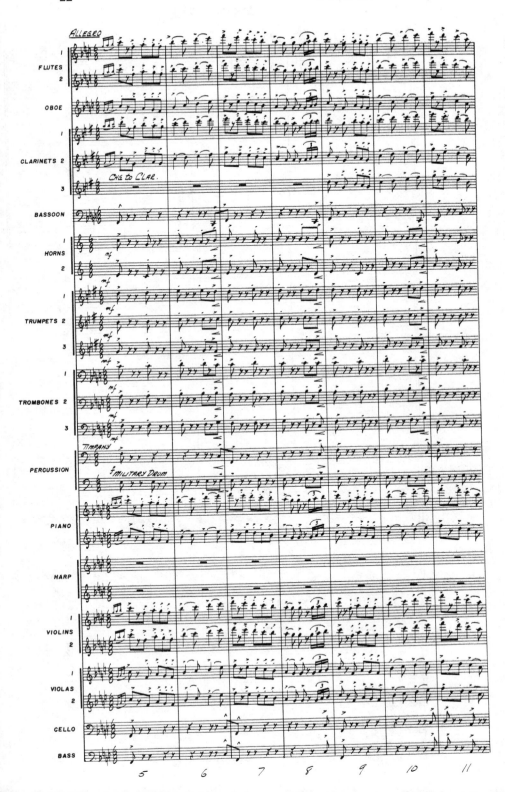

(For lack of space the complete sketch and score is not shown. This is sufficient, however, for purposes of study.)

After I had finished the main title, I reviewed the next scene, I-B. The scene was a direct segue from the title music.

When this happens, the keys of the music have to be the same or related so that in the final dubbing, the music is correct when the mixer dials in the incoming music track.

The following is the timing sheet of I-B:

MUSIC I-B   "THE IRISHMAN"
                        O'Toole

Establishing shot: O'Toole walking through countryside.

.00   Start to fade in on M.L.S. of O'Toole walking, camera right, silhouetted against the sky.

.02   Fade full in.

.04⅓   O'Toole stops walking and turns toward camera, smiling.

.08⅓   O'Toole starts to jump down from wall toward camera.

.09   He lands, starts to walk toward camera.

.10⅔   He walks gaily.

.14⅓   He tosses his shillelagh in the air.

.15⅓   He catches it.

(.18) He stops under apple tree, he looks up.

.20⅔   He raises his shillelagh up and swings it.

.22⅓   Cut to C.U. as he throws his shillelagh in tree.

.23⅓   An apple drops into scene. He catches it.

.24⅓   His shillelagh drops into scene. He catches it.

.24⅔   He raises the apple to his mouth.

(.25⅔) He takes a bite and starts to walk right, camera dollies with him.

.28⅓   Start to fade in on first superimposed foreword:
           "TO THIS WANDERER THE GREEN LAND OF IRELAND MEANT PEACE AND QUIET."

.32   O'Toole tosses shillelagh into the air.

.33   He catches it.

.36   Fade out on first foreword.

(.38⅓) Start to fade in on second foreword:
           "BUT TO OTHERS, IRELAND WAS A BACKGROUND FOR PLOTS, INTRIGUE AND VIOLENCE."   etc.

The timing sheet contiued and described the balance of the scene, ending at one minute and fifty-one seconds (1.51).

It is best to consult the glossary for meanings of abbreviations that refer to motion picture terms or slang.

After studying the timing sheet, I decided to repeat the principal theme in gay form at the beginning. As the main title ended in B flat, I could start this scene in the relative key of F. It should be lighter in sound, and it should also be orchestrated differently, the wood-winds alone on the melody and the strings on the chords in place of the brass.

I determined a tempo of four bars for three and a half seconds (.03½).

I continued with this treatment until I arrived at eighteen seconds (.18), the first important cue. At twenty-five and two-thirds seconds (.25⅔) was another important cue, and at thirty-eight and one-third (.38⅓) was a very important cue.

I-B   O'TOOLE

A humorous section appears here with a tempo change as O'Toole stops under the tree; this also has a pastorale feeling.

It segues into the broad treatment under the first foreword, ". . . green land of Ireland . . ." etc.

A very decided change appears at thirty-eight and one-third seconds (.38 1/3) . . . ominous and with the menace theme introduced for the first time, under the second foreword, ". . . Ireland was a background for plots, . . ." etc.

After this was orchestrated, I studied the timing sheet of I-C:

"THE IRISHMAN"
O'Toole Meets Maureen

Establishing shot: Music segues from I-B on cut to M.S. of Lord Stanhope astride his horse. We see Kitty seated in B. G.

0.00	Music starts to M.S. of Lord Stanhope astride his horse. Kitty in B.G.
0.00⅔	Stanhope says: "Mr. Hendrigg."
0.01	Pause.
0.03	Hendrigg enters scene and stops, looking up at Stanhope.
0.04	Stanhope says: "I want you to make certain." Camera moves in slowly.
0.05	Hendrigg interrupts saying: "I suggest, sir, you return to Dublin at once. You might be seen. I'll follow and report to you there the moment this is over." As he starts to speak, camera holds on M.L.S.
0.01⅔	Pause.
0.11⅓	Stanhope says: "Don't fail."
(0.12⅓)	Pause. Stanhope wheels his horse and rides away, as Kitty and Hendrigg watch.
0.15⅓	Kitty asks: "Why did he leave me here?"
0.16⅔	Hendrigg starts to walk toward Kitty. Camera moves in following him.
0.17⅔	Hendrigg says: "You have work to do, be quiet."
(0.19⅓)	Cut to M.L.S., Jack and Pat as they mount their horses. Pat says: "Travelers from England always carry plenty of money."
0.22	Hendrigg from O.S. says: "None of that." Camera pans left.
0.23	We see Hendrigg standing beside Pat's horse.

0.23⅔   Hendrigg continues: "You hold the horses and nothing else." Camera holds on M.3 S.

0.27   Pat says: "Yes, sir."

0.27⅔   Jack says: "Aye, sir."

0.28⅓   Cut to M.L.S. of Kitty as she walks forward, camera moving with her, she says: "I don't like him. What does General Bonaparte want here in Ireland?"

0.31   Kitty is still speaking as we start to see three men.

0.32⅔   Kitty stops in front of Hendrigg, as camera continues to pull back. Hendrigg says: "Don't ask so many questions."

(0.35)   Pause. Camera holds on M.S. of the group. We hear a carriage horn from O.S.

0.35⅓   The group react, turning their heads.

0.36   Cut to M.S., shooting over horses heads as they pull carriage, running. We see trumpeter still blowing carriage horn.

(0.38⅔)   Cut to M.S. of group looking O.S., as Hendrigg says: "Quickly now."

0.39⅔   Pat and Jack ride out of scene fast, as camera starts to move in.

0.42⅔   Kitty says: "Oh, Mr. Hendrigg, you're stepping on a shamrock."

0.45   Kitty continues: "It's bad luck, you know."

0.47   Hendrigg speaks: "Keep quiet."

(0.48⅓)   Cut to L.S. of carriage, as Pat and Jack ride toward the carriage.   etc.

After studying this timing, I could see that the kidnap plot was beginning to unfold. Lord Stanhope was the Englishman plotting with the thugs and Mr. Hendrigg, the chief plotter.

As this was a direct segue from the I-B music which ended thus:

I should start this music with the menace theme.

The first important cue was at 12⅓ seconds.

The second important cue was at 19⅓ seconds.

The third important cue was at 35 seconds.

The fourth important cue was at 38⅔ seconds.

The fifth important cue was at 48⅓ seconds.

In this particular sequence there were many dialogue scenes for which music was to be written. The music, therefore, should not be too heavy, or it would interfere with the dialogue.

I would write a musical effect for the carriage horn using French horns or trumpets with the felt hat.

As I started to write, the sketch looked like this:

O'TOOLE MEETS MAUREEN

By comparing the sketch with the timing sheet, you see the menace theme in the bass. Added, in the first bar, is a snare drum and tympani effect.

In bars three and four are the horns and trombones.

For the first cue at twelve and one-third seconds (0.12⅓) a phrase is written for full orchestra as Stanhope rides away, with a diminuendo for the dialogue at fifteen and one-third seconds (0.15⅓). Here Kitty says, "Why did he leave me here?" rather sadly, so an English horn phrase is written.

At nineteen and one-third seconds (0.19⅓) is a cut to the thugs. Ominous chords are employed in the lower register. The snare drum and tympani effect reappears.

At thirty-five seconds (0.35) the carriage horn effect appears.

At thirty-eight and two-thirds seconds (0.38⅔) is a cut to the group of thugs and Hendrigg says, "Quickly, now." The full orchestra starts after the down-beat of the bar (in other words, after he has spoken his line) with an exciting movement as Pat and Jack ride away. This is marked "Piu Mosso," or fast at two seconds a bar.

By checking the sketch, you can see that the first two bars are at a tempo of four seconds a bar, with the fourth bar at about three seconds, then back to four seconds a bar until bar nine which is three and two-thirds seconds (.03⅔). Bars eleven and twelve are two seconds a bar.

At forty-two and two-thirds seconds (.042⅔) Kitty speaks dialogue. So that the music does not interfere with that dialogue, only a high string tremolo and English horn are written for these two bars. There is also a tempo adjustment, Meno Mosso, for two reasons: (1) It allows the conductor ample time to prepare for the next important cue at forty-eight and two-thirds seconds (0.48⅔), and (2) Under dialogue an effective device in dramatic scenes is sustained chords. These are flexible for the conductor when recording and are a means of modulation.

The following is the orchestration of the sketch:

O'TOOLE MEETS MAUREEN

I-C

When I arrived at this point in the sketch, a chase and a fight started so I continued with generally exciting music as the thugs stopped the carriage, trying to kidnap Maureen. O'Toole at this moment arrived on the scene, threw his club which hit one of the thugs on the head, and then jumped on him. After subduing them, O'Toole walked over to Maureen.

I consulted the timing sheet at about one minute and forty-one seconds (1.41) and found that it read:

MUSIC 1-C   "THE IRISHMAN"
O'Toole Meets Maureen (Cont.)

1.41	G.U. of O'Toole.
1.42	He draws his arm back.
1.43	He throws his shillelagh.
(1.44⅓)	Shillelagh hits thug on the head.
(1.48⅓)	O'Toole lands on thug.
1.49⅓	He jumps and runs toward Maureen.
1.51⅔	O'Toole picks up pistol and holds it on Jack.
1.53	He looks toward Maureen.
1.53⅔	He smiles and says: "Ah, good afternoon. My name's O'Toole."
1.57	O'Toole tosses the gun into his other hand.
1.57⅔	Cut to C.S. O'Toole and Maureen.
1.58⅓	O'Toole bows and says: "Your servant."
1.59⅔	Maureen turns and looks O.S.
2.00	She screams: "Watch out."
2.01	Cut to C.S. of Jack as he starts to throw a knife.
2.01⅔	We hear a knife land in wood.
(2.02)	Cut to M.C.S. Knife sticking in the door of the carriage between them.
2.03	O'Toole looks camera right, angrily.
2.04	O'Toole starts forward, camera pans with him.
2.05⅓	O'Toole grabs Jack and says: "Where's your manners."
(2.06⅓)	He hits Jack on chin.
2.07	He lands on the ground.
2.07⅔	Cut to C.U. of O'Toole as he laughs, turns and walks toward Maureen.
(2.09⅔)	He says to Maureen: "No sense of gallantry at all." etc.

After studying the timing I decided that I wanted to catch the club hitting the thug on the head, O'Toole landing on the thug, the knife in the carriage, the blow on the chin, and the fall on the ground.

A note here may help to clear up why the complete action is timed.

It may seem that there is much unnecessary description of the scenes, but for the music writer it is a tremendous help to see all the complete action and dialogue, though he only catches certain cues.

After reviewing the picture carefully before writing, these notes enable the composer to remember the scene in all its details and make it possible to write the score away from the picture and the studio.

I then proceeded with the sketch and wrote the following:

I-C   O'TOOLE MEETS MAUREEN (Cont'd.)

The analysis of this sketch shows a full orchestra chord played when O'Toole hits the thug, then it is sustained in the basses.

At one minute and forty-eight and one-third seconds (1.48 ⅓) as O'Toole lands on Jack, a full orchestra movement is employed. It is not dramatic, but in a rather rollicking mood.

At bar 91, the quarter notes give flexibility to hit the important cue at two minutes and two seconds (2.02) where the knife is seen.

At bar 94, two accented chords are played as O'Toole hits the thug on the chin—the first chord for the blow on the jaw and the second for the fall to the ground.

At bar 95 the mood changes to O'Toole's character, carefree and rather gay.

The following is the orchestration of the preceding sketch:

FLUTES 1 2
OBOE
CLARINETS 1 2 3
BASS CLAR
BASSOON
HORNS 1 2
TRUMPETS 1 2 3
TROMBONES 1 2 3
PERCUSSION
TIMPS
DRUMS
PIANO
HARP
VIOLINS 1 2
VIOLAS 1 2
CELLO
BASS
79 80 81 82 83 84 85 86

Composer's Sketch and Stop Watch

Establishing shot: Music segues from I-D on middle of dissolve to Hendrigg, Kitty and the two "heavies."

MUSIC 1-D   "THE IRISHMAN"
                      Maureen

0.00   Music starts on middle of Diss. to M.S. of Hendrigg, Kitty and the heavies.

0.01⅓   Hendrigg speaks with disgust: "Bungling! He's only one man and unarmed."

0.04⅓ Hendrigg continues: "Remember, I pay you for results only."

0.06⅓ Kitty says: "It's going to rain. Let's go back to Dublin."

0.08⅔ Hendrigg says: "Not yet."

0.09⅓ Hendrigg speaks to Pat and Jack, saying: "Go now, we'll try again at the hill road."

(0.11) Jack starts to ride out. Pat turns his horse.

(0.13) Middle of dissolve from Hendrigg to M.L.S. of carriage running, camera right, camera pans with it.

(0.17⅓) Middle of Diss. from L.S. of carriage of C.2 S. of O'Toole and Maureen inside the carriage. Maureen has her head on O'Toole's shoulder. She is still in a faint.

0.21⅓ Maureen moves her head, straightens up with a start.

0.22⅓ She looks at O'Toole.

0.22⅔ She turns her head and looks out of the carriage.

0.24⅔ She looks back at O'Toole.

0.26 O'Toole says: "Don't fret."

0.26⅔ He hands her her purse saying: "Here's your money."

0.28⅓ Maureen takes purse, saying, "Thank you."

0.30 Maureen says: "Where are you taking me?" etc.

After a study of the timing, I planned to open this scene with menace under the dialogue of Hendrigg and the heavies. At eleven seconds (0.11) Jack started to ride out.

At thirteen seconds (0.13) there was a dissolve to a nice shot of the carriage in a medium long shot (M.L.S.) which was a chance for about four bars of music in the open without any dialogue to worry about.

At seventeen and one-third seconds (0.17⅓) the scene dissolved to the inside of the carriage—a good place to introduce the love melody for the first time in the picture.

After I had started on the sketch, it looked like this:

I-D   MAUREEN

In analyzing this sketch we find a slight variation of the menace theme.

At eleven seconds (0.11) the horns and trombones play a figuration, as Jack starts to ride out, which leads into the cue and a change of mood at thirteen seconds (0.13).

Notice that the tempo of the first two bars is at four (4) seconds a bar. Bar 3 is in three (3) seconds a bar which is marked "Poco Accel." Bar 4 is in 2/4 tempo. This provides a slight accelerando to arrive gracefully at the brighter tempo at thirteen seconds (0.13).

As you are writing to a measured piece of film, you are confined to writing music to that same footage or measure-ment—hence, the sudden change to a 2/4 bar in this sketch.

Beginning at thirteen seconds (0.13) the music is written with a pastorale feeling. The strings and horns have a melodic line in three octaves, while the trumpets and wood-winds have a rhythmic pattern that portrays a feeling of galloping.

At seventeen and one-third seconds (0.17⅓) the next important cue occurs. Here the color changes and is light in character. The love theme starts to appear in the wood-winds with a light string accompaniment.

At twenty-six and one-third seconds (0.26⅓) the dialogue starts. This scene continued with the love theme. Played by the strings to the end of the scene which occurred at 2.00⅔.

The following is the orchestration of this sketch:

MAUREEN

I-D

After completing I-D, I started to study I-E.

In the story, the carriage stopped for O'Toole to get out while Maureen continued on to Dublin. O'Toole crossed the fields in a happy mood because he was on the way to his castle, which he hadn't seen in years.

The timing sheet read:

MUSIC 1-E   "THE IRISHMAN"
                     Castle O'Toole

Establishing shot: Music starts on cut to Maureen inside the carriage.

0.00	Music starts on C.U. of Maureen in carriage.
0.00⅔	Maureen reacts, looks up and out the window.
0.02⅔	Her expression changes, there is going to be a storm.
0.06⅓	She reaches forward and picks up her bonnet.
(0.07⅔)	Cut to M.S. of O'Toole. He tosses his shillelagh in the air, catches it, starts to walk away from camera, rapidly, very gay.
0.13	He spreads his arms out in happiness.
(0.19⅔)	Middle of Dissolve from O'Toole walking away from camera to extreme L.S. of the Castle O'Toole. Camera is shooting across fields toward the castle, that is silhouetted against a stormy sky.
0.20⅔	O'Toole walks into scene from behind camera.
0.22⅓	He stops in C.S. looking toward the castle.
0.22⅔	Cut to M.C.U. of O'Toole as he looks proudly toward castle.
0.23⅓	He shouts, "Castle O'Toole." He stretches his arms out as he says this. etc.

As I studied this timing, I decided to open it with the love theme over the cut of Maureen.

At seven and two-thirds seconds (0.07⅔) the mood should be gay, maybe a scherzo, because O'Toole was going to see his boyhood home once more. Then, too, he had just met a very charming girl.

At nineteen and two-thirds seconds (0.19⅔), I decided the principal theme, in broad treatment, would be good as the castle was revealed in the background. The music would thus have dignity in relation to the majesty of the old castle.

When I started to write, the sketch looked like this:

In the analysis of this sketch, you will see the love theme in the strings.

Beginning at seven and two-thirds seconds (0.07⅔), when the picture cuts to O'Toole starting to walk gaily, there is a scherzo movement based upon the principal theme. It is played by the wood-winds, while the strings play a pizzicato background. The tempo of this section is one (1) second to the bar.

This continues up to the cue at nineteen and two-thirds seconds (0.19⅔), where the picture cuts to the long shot of the castle. With a crescendo in bar 13, the music resolves to another key and the principal theme is employed in a broad or noble version. This scene continued to thirty-five seconds (0.35) and stopped when O'Toole reached the castle.

The following example is the score, which will show how the strings are divided in the pizzicato movement.

CASTLE O'TOOLE

I-E

I had now completed the first reel.

The next scene to write was a change-over scene. As the scene really started in the last few feet of Reel I, the music cutter would have to cut that portion of the scene from Reel I and splice it onto the beginning of the next reel (Reel II) for recording. He could also build this scene as a unit alone (a reel in itself) by lifting or cutting that portion of the scene from Reel II and splicing it onto the small piece cut from Reel I and then mounting this film on a separate, small reel; when we recorded, the scene would thus be intact to show on the screen of the recording stage.

Studying the sketch, I could see some action starting. As the story progressed, Maureen stopped the carriage and sent her footman ahead to see how bad the storm was. He hurried back to tell her that there were some highwaymen up ahead, though actually they were really Hendrigg's thugs waiting for her to pass. Maureen's coachman decided to take her back to O'Toole's castle, so Jack and Pat started to chase her.

The timing sheet read like this:

MUSIC 1-F & 2-A   "THE IRISHMAN"
                 A Run for Safety

0.00	Music starts on middle of dissolve to L.S. of roadway. We see the coachman running toward camera, camera pulls back.
0.01⅓	We start to see the horses.
0.03⅓	We see the carriage as the coachman runs up.
(0.04)	We see Maureen in the carriage as camera holds on M.C.S. The coachman stops and says: "There are two horsemen beyond the hill."
0.06⅓	Maureen says: "Drive through."
0.07⅔	The coachman replies: "We can't risk it."
0.09	The coachman starts to close the door as he says: "We're turning back."
(0.10)	He slams the door and starts to run, camera right.
0.12⅔	He grabs the bridle of the lead horse, starts to turn them around.
0.15	(REEL II) Cut to 2 S. of Pat and Jack as they sit on their horses, masks over their eyes.

0.16⅓   They react.

0.17⅔   Jack says: "Come on."

⟨0.18⅔⟩ They start out fast.

0.19⅓   Cut to M.L.S. as Jack and Pat come out of trees
         and ride down hill toward camera.

0.22   Jack rides past camera.

⟨0.23⅓⟩ Cut to extreme L.S. of carriage coming down the
         road, camera left, camera is shooting from above.

This scene I thought should start with a little excitement, as the coachman ran back to the carriage. There should be a little suspense under the dialogue at four seconds (0.04) and at ten seconds (0.10) *REAL* excitement. (Notice at fifteen seconds (0.15) the reel splice occurs from Reel I to Reel II.)

At fifteen seconds (0.15) there should be suspense under the shot of Jack and Pat, and at eighteen and two-thirds seconds (0.18⅔) they started to ride out fast.

After starting the sketch, it looked like this:

A RUN FOR SAFETY

*In analyzing the sketch, you will note a string and wood-
wind passage as the coachman runs. At four seconds (0.04)
the tempo slows down (Meno)—the character of the music is
one of suspense.*

*Beginning at ten seconds (0.10) the excitement starts.
The tempo is fast, four bars of "Alla Breve" in five (5) seconds. From fifteen seconds (0.15) to eighteen and two-thirds
seconds (0.18⅔), the tempo relaxes under the shot of Pat and
Jack. With the horns and trombones, the "G's" will sound
ominous.*

*At eighteen and two-thirds seconds (0.18⅔) the excite-
ment recurs.*

I continued with this scene as Maureen's carriage raced
back to the castle. There she got out, rushed through the courtyard and hid behind a wall, waiting for a chance to run to
the castle.

At fifty-two and two-thirds seconds (0.52⅔) the picture
cut to O'Toole inside the castle inspecting his old home. He
finally arrived at a corner filled with some toys, which re-
minded him of his childhood.

The timing sheet continued as follows:

MUSIC 1-F & 2-A   "THE IRISHMAN"

A Run for Safety (Cont.)

(0.52⅔) Middle of dissolve from Maureen in courtyard
            to O'Toole in castle. He is inspecting some toys
            that remind him of his childhood.

0.55   He turns and looks at a picture.

0.57⅓   He walks over to it.

(1.00⅓) He reaches for it.

1.02   He takes hold of it.

1.08   He turns to walk back to the toys.

1.13⅔   He picks up a small wagon.

1.16⅔   He starts to walk forward, slowly.

1.21   Camera starts to move back.

1.24⅓   He stops walking, looking camera right.   etc.

At fifty-two and two-thirds seconds (0.52⅔) on the dissolve to O'Toole in the castle, I planned to have a neutral type of music. At one minute and one-third second (1.00⅓) I wanted to have a child effect as O'Toole reminisced about his childhood.

After reaching this point in the sketch, it looked like this:

Analyzing this sketch, you will find that bars 40 and 41 are neutral music. At one minute and one-third second (1.00⅓) the strings resolve to a chord over which the celeste plays a music-box effect of the principal theme.

The score was progressing at a much faster pace by now. With every day the writing became more fun than work.

After finishing 2-A I started to study 2-B. As the story continued, Maureen finally made her way to the castle and was admitted by O'Toole. They went in to sit by the fireplace and talk.

The timing sheet read:

MUSIC 2-B   "THE IRISHMAN"
                    O'Toole's Love

0.00	Music starts at middle of dissolve to M.2 S. of O'Toole and Maureen seated before fire.
0.00⅔	O'Toole says: "And so for years I have wandered over the world."
0.05⅔	O'Toole continues: "—soldiering for any foreign country that would pay me."
0.07⅔	Pause.
0.08⅓	Dialogue continues.
0.10⅔	He pauses.
0.12⅓	Cut to C.2 S. from behind Maureen. O'Toole says: "Now everything is changed."
0.13⅔	Pause.
0.15	O'Toole says: "For the first time I have a reason for doing things."
0.17	Pause.
0.18	O'Toole says: "You."
0.18⅔	Cut to reverse shot. Maureen says: "I'm to be married soon."
0.27	Cut to reverse angle. O'Toole says: "I'll win you somehow."
0.29	Cut to reverse angle. Maureen says: "It's impossible."
0.31⅔	Maureen reaches for her muff as she says: "Come, we must be going."
0.33	Cut to M.C.S. as they both get up.

0.45   Maureen turns and walks toward her wrap.

0.48   We hear a knock on the door.

0.49   Cut to M.S. of door as O'Toole opens it.   etc.

After studying the timing sheet, I decided I could ignore the dialogue and just play the love theme with strings. At forty-eight seconds (0.48), there should be a change of mood.

The sketch looked like this after it had been written:

2-B   O'TOOLE'S LOVE

*In the analysis of this sketch you can see a simple treat-
ment of the love theme with muted strings alone.*

*At forty-eight seconds (0.48) a knock on the door changes
the mood. Instead of the chord resolving to the tonic of the
key of E Major, it resolves to an ominous chord. As the knock
on the door interrupts the mood of a sweet, friendly scene, the
ominous chord interrupts the mood of the music. This gives
a feeling of suspense and that something threatening is in
the offing. This chord is effective if sustained for a length of
time and then gradually faded out.*

*A note at this time may be helpful about the "fading out"
of music at the end of a scene. By resolving to the tonic chord
at the close of a scene, it is more obvious to the listener that
the music is completed. By finishing with an unresolved chord,
however, the listener is not so conscious that the music is
coming to a close. The over-all effect of many scenes, such
as love or intimate dialogue scenes, is achieved by writing
the music so that it will "fade in" and "fade out" without
any conscious reaction on the part of the listener.*

The story had now progressed to the place where the
French countess arrived. I would use the pizzicato movement
for her tripping into the tavern. The timing sheet was not
detailed, but what we call an "over-all." As the scene was
only one of general excitement of the countess' arriving, there
was no need of a detailed description. In this type of timing
sheet only the important cues are timed, for example:

MUSIC 2-C   "THE IRISHMAN"
                       The Countess

0.00   Music starts on the coachman announcing the
          Countess.

0.44   Camera stops, panning on the Countess' shapely
          legs as she gets out of the carriage.   etc.

When I started to write this scene employing the short
theme I had written, it looked like this:

2-C

THE COUNTESS

*In analyzing this sketch you will note a full string pizzi-
cato movement at an allegro tempo, one second to the bar.
This continues in strict tempo until the cue at forty-four seconds (0.44) where a sustained chord with a harp embellish-
ment appears as the Countess starts to get out of the carriage.*

*At bar 47, a violin passage starts over her movements as
she looks everyone over.*

*At bar 49, she says, "Delightful, delightful, delightful."
A wood-wind figure answers her in a mocking way.*

*In the following orchestration of Scene 2-C, note the
division of the strings:*

2-C

THE COUNTESS

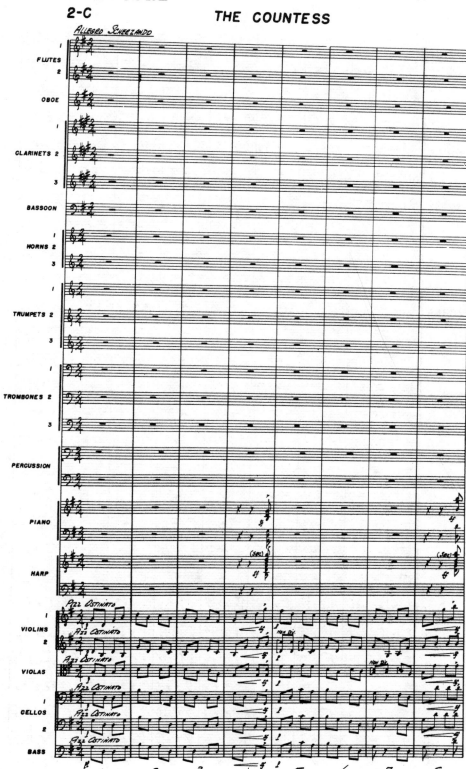

FLUTES
OBOE
CLARINETS
BASSOON
HORNS
TRUMPETS
TROMBONES
PERCUSSION
TRIANGLE
PIANO
HARP
VIOLINS
VIOLAS
CELLOS
BASS
17
18
19
20
21
22
23
24
25

FLUTES 1 2
OBOE
CLARINETS 1 2 3
BASSOON
HORNS 1 2 3
TRUMPETS 1 2 3
TROMBONES 1 2 3
PERCUSSION
PIANO
HARP
VIOLINS 1 2
VIOLAS
CELLOS 1 2
BASS
CRESC POCO A POCO
35 36 37 38 39 40 41 42 43 44

I continued with this scene to the end, with the pizzicato movement as she entered the tavern. The final length of the scene was two minutes, thirty-two and one-third seconds (2.32⅓).

There was still one more scene to do in Reel II. It was about the English couple in the diplomatic service. In the story they would meet in the gardens and would plan their future together—they would have a farm in England and be very happy.

I wrote the following pastorale theme to underscore this mood:

I continued this scene until I reached one minute and forty-four seconds (1.44). Here I came to a very important section of the timing. Katie and Charles had quarreled, and after he had left her, she started to look for him in the barn. A little later he returned, and they kissed and made up.

I studied this portion of the timing sheet, as follows:

MUSIC 2-D   "THE IRISHMAN"

Katie and Charles (Cont.)

1.44   Cut to Katie, standing in the garden, searching for Charles.

1.47½   She looks off in the direction of the roadway.

1.49   She turns to her left and starts to run toward the barn. Camera panning with her.

1:54   She stops at a stall, looks off in the distance.

1.59   Her body relaxes disappointedly as she turns slowly back to the garden.

2.06⅓   She starts to resume her slow walk back to the garden.

2.09⅓   She pauses as she catches sight of a swinging doorway in the barn.

2.11   She starts to walk quickly, then breaks into a run.

(2.14)   She reaches the door as we cut to reverse C.S.
          of her entering the stable.
2.15   She pauses sharply at the doorway.
2.19½   She pauses and hopelessly shakes her head.
2.23½   A hopeful thought strikes her as she moves toward
          the window.
2.26⅓   She leans over and peers out. The wind is blow-
          ing very hard.
2.28⅓   She gives a forceful push at the window, then
          peers out.
2.31⅓   She gives another push.
2.32   Up-stage we see Charles behind her.
2.33⅓   Charles says: "Could you use an extra man?"
2.35   Katie's face shows a remarkable change.
2.36   Katie says: "Charles."
2.37   Slight pause. The window weaves back and forth.
2.38⅓   Charles says: "I forgot how I said it before."
2.40   Charles leaps over the wall.
2.42   He lands and starts to walk toward Katie.
2.43⅓   He stretches his arms out happily, Katie runs
          to him.
(2.45⅓)   He clasps her eagerly.
2.55⅔   The barn window blows shut.
2.57⅓   Start to fade out.
3.00   Fade full out.

At one minute and forty-nine seconds (1.49) she started
for the barn. As her thoughts were on Charles, I started the
love theme.

At two minutes and fourteen seconds (2.14) she reached
the door, disappointed. Here the music should be emotional.

At two minutes, forty-three and one-third seconds (2.43⅓)
Katie started to run to him, and they kissed at two minutes,
forty-five and one–third seconds (2.45⅓). I would try to
catch this action.

After writing the sketch, it looked like this:

KATIE & CHARLES (Cont'd.)

*In the analysis of the sketch, you can see that the tim-
ing picks up at one minute, and forty-nine seconds (1.49).
Here as Katie starts toward the barn, the love theme commences. This describes her feelings and thoughts. At bars 43
and 44 the melody and the harmonic construction is such that
it gives a feeling of disappointment and sadness.*

*At two minutes and fourteen seconds (2.14) she reaches
the door and enters. The high strings will be very emotional
here. In bar 48 the flute and oboe sustain a note throughout
the bar. This serves two purposes; it gives a feeling of suspense,
and here the Sound Department will add a wind effect which
will combined well with the musical effect. The strings enter
again in bar 49, and the same sustained effect is repeated in
bar 50. On the fourth beat of bar 54, the strings start a run
which reaches a climax on the kiss at two minutes, forty-five
and one-third seconds (2.45⅓). As the barn door swings back
and forth, the melody is completed.*

The orchestra score was written as follows:

2-D   KATIE & CHARLES (Cont'd)

I now had two reels completed. As I glanced over the timing sheets, I discovered that there was only one music cue in Reel III; the balance of the reel contained action which did not require underscoring.

The scene in Reel III using music was one with Kitty and O'Toole in which he told her the pixies were talking in order to detain her—a scene having a sense of humor.

The timing sheet was as follows:

MUSIC 3-A   "THE IRISHMAN"
                            Pixies

0.00   Music starts after O'Toole says: "Hear the voices?"
0.00⅔   Pause. Kitty looks down slowly at the table, beginning to look frightened.
0.01⅔   O'Toole continues: "He's the wisest pixie of the lot." As he says this, Kitty looks up at him, her eyes wide with terror.
0.03⅔   Pause.
0.04⅓   O'Toole says: "Shh! He's talking."
0.05   Pause. O'Toole leans down, as if listening.
(0.06)   Cut to C.U. of Kitty, she glances down at the table, frightened.
0.07⅔   She speaks: "I don't hear anything."
0.09⅔   Cut to M.C.U. of O'Toole as he raises his hand to quiet her.
0.10⅓   He looks down at the table, listening.
0.12   O'Toole says: "No."
0.14   O'Toole says: "Oh, no, you can't do that."
(0.16)   Pause.
0.17   O'Toole sighs.
0.19   O'Toole says: "Pixies are funny people."
0.22   Pause.
0.22⅓   Cut to C.U. of Kitty, her eyes wide with fear.
0.22⅔   O'Toole says: "He says he knows about you. He's going to cast a spell."
0.26   Kitty exclaims: "A spell!"
0.27⅓   Kitty starts to stand up.
0.27⅔   Cut to 2.S. Kitty says: "On me?"
0.30   O'Toole says: "Yes."

(0.33⅔) Cut to 2 S. as she gasps in horror.

0.34⅔ She looks at table.

(0.36⅔) She raises her hand.

0.37 She licks her finger.

0.37⅔ She crosses her fingers.

0.38 She looks at O'Toole, her eyes wide with terror.

0.40⅔ Kitty says: "Tell them to stop."

0.42⅔ Cut to M.C.2 S. O'Toole raises his hand to silence her.

0.44⅔ His head is low, listening.

(0.48⅔) O'Toole says: "What's your name?"   etc.

As I studied the timing sheet, I decided to play this scene for comedy. I would imitate a voice with an instrument and try to emphasize Kitty's fear. I would also use Kitty's theme in a humorous manner.

When I started writing the sketch, it looked like this:

3-A

PIXIE

In the analysis of this sketch, you will see an orchestral arrangement at the start which creates a slightly weird effect. A soft tremolo is written for the violins, with a viola pizzicato and harp playing seconds.

As O'Toole says, "Hear the voices?" the bassoon answers playing a humorous passage to imitate a voice talking.

At six seconds (0.06) Kitty is frightened, so the violas and the wood-winds play a trilling passage.

At sixteen (0.16) seconds as she looks up, the bassoon starts her theme, which is played in a humorous mood.

At thirty-three seconds (0.33) she starts to get very frightened, so a trilling effect starts and reaches its peak at thirty-six and two-thirds seconds (0.36⅔).

This scene continued until one minute, thirty-two and one-third seconds (1.32⅓) had elapsed, with the music written in the same vein—as light and as funny as possible.

I was now ready to start work on Reel IV. The timing sheet revealed to me that some excitement was about to begin.

As the story unfolded, O'Toole was bringing Maureen to her father's house in Dublin in the morning. As they entered the street, the thugs were waiting in hiding, still endeavoring to kidnap Maureen. Hendrigg was in Stanhope's house, and together they were watching the proceedings from a window. The timing sheet was as follows:

MUSIC 4-A   "THE IRISHMAN"
                         Ambush

0.00	Music starts on Hendrigg and Stanhope looking out of the window.
0.02⅔	Cut to three men on the street corner.
0.09	Cut to 2 S. Hendrigg waving to men.
0.13⅓	Cut to inside of house.
0.14	Dialogue.
0.19⅓	Stanhope pats Hendrigg on the shoulder.
(0.27)	Middle of dissolve to Maureen and O'Toole, riding in a cart.
0.33⅔	Cut to M.L.S. of men in street.
(0.50½)	Cut to Pat.
(0.53½)	Cut to L.S. of street.

(0.57½) Cut to O'Toole and Maureen.
(1.00½) Cut to M.S. O'Toole starts to urge the horse for-
         ward.
1.03⅔   Cut to C.S. O'Toole swinging the whip.
1.08¼   Cut to M.S. the men holding O'Toole, they strug-
         gle.
1.18⅔   They try to grab Maureen.
1.21⅓   O'Toole starts to jump into the air.
1.21¾   He kicks one thug in the jaw.

As this was the start of the fight, we decided to stop this cue here and start the next scene, 4-B, on the sock to the jaw. Long pieces of music are tiring for the orchestra to record, hence we often split a long scene into several sections of music.

After studying the timing sheet, I decided to open the scene with the menace theme.

At twenty-seven seconds (0.27) where the picture cut to O'Toole in the cart, I would use a mood of suspense or of something foreboding.

At fifty and one-half seconds (0.50½), fifty-three and one-half seconds (0.53½), and fifty-seven and one-half seconds (0.57½) were three cuts between the thugs and O'Toole, each one of which I would punctuate.

At one minute and one-half second (1.00½) the action began, so I planned to start some music which would build into the following scene, 4-B.

After I had written the sketch, it looked like this:

4-A

AMBUSH

In analyzing this sketch, you will notice the menace theme at the beginning.

At twenty-seven seconds (0.27), where we see O'Toole in the cart, a tremolo starts softly for suspense while a pizzicato passage appears in the bass.

At fifty and one-half seconds (0.50½), fifty-three and one-half seconds (0.53½), and fifty-seven and one-half seconds (0.57½), where the picture cuts back and forth, each cut is punctuated with a change of chord, slightly accented.

At one minute and one-half second (1.00½), an agitato starts with the violins and violas. This is constructed with imitation phrases in the basses. At bar 24 the volume starts to pick up, which will lead into the next scene, 4-B.

As this sketch is very clear orchestrally, no score will be shown.

As I started to write 4-B, I realized that it would have to commence with a chord that would resolve from the last chord in 4-A, in order to make a direct segue from 4-A to 4-B.

Studying the timing sheet, I saw that it was a general fight and did not have too many direct cues to hit. The timing sheet read:

MUSIC 4-B   "THE IRISHMAN"

Plan Foiled

0.00   Music starts as O'Toole kicks thug.
0.02   Cut to C.S. as thug falls away.
0.03⅔   O'Toole hits another thug a terrific jolt on the jaw.
0.05⅔   Cut to M.L.S. O'Toole jumps into cart.
0.08¼   Cut to thugs running toward O'Toole.
0.11½   Cut to C.S. O'Toole grabs rope.
0.13⅔   Cut to M.S. O'Toole raises himself.
0.14⅓   One of the men swing at him.
0.14⅔   He kicks the man out of the scene.   etc.

After studying the timing sheet, I decided to catch one important cue, and for the remainder of the scene, I would write general fight music.

As scene 4-A had ended with the chord:

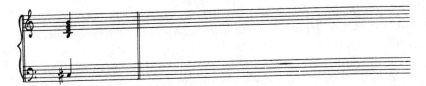

I decided to start scene 4-B with an F minor chord:

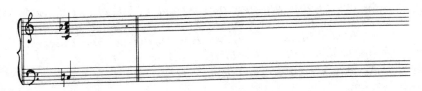

The sound of this chord would give the music a lift and a fresh start into the actual fight. I also planned that the fight music should not be written too seriously, perhaps in a 6/8 tempo, so that it would sound rollicking. In other words, O'Toole was having a good time.

After I wrote the sketch, it looked like this:

In the analysis of this sketch, you will see that the brass has an accented chord on the down-beat where O'Toole kicks the thug.

The only cue which has been pointed up is at three and two-thirds seconds (0.03⅔), where O'Toole socks the thug on the jaw.

In bar 3, the horns play a variation of the principal theme.

At bar 9, the trumpets start a phrase with an Irish flavor in the minor, which is imitated in the basses starting at bar 11.

This same vein of writing was continued to the end of the cue at two minutes and four seconds (2.04).

The following is the score of 4-B:

4-B

PLAN FOILED

FLUTES 1 2
OBOE
CLARINETS 1 2 3
BASSOON
HORNS 1 2
TRUMPETS 1 2 3
TROMBONES 1 2 3
PERCUSSION
PIANO
HARP
VIOLINS 1 2
VIOLAS 1 2
CELLO
BASS
9 10 11 12 13 14 15 16

Now I had four reels completed, and, as I looked over the timing sheet of scene 5-A, I saw that it was a light, humorous scene. In the story, O'Toole went to a tailor shop to be fitted for a captain's uniform; he posed while the tailor put on the finishing touches here and there.

The timing sheet read:

MUSIC 5-A   "THE IRISHMAN"

Captain O'Toole

0.00   Music starts on fade in to tailor shop.
0.02   Full fade in. O'Toole is dressed in a captain's uniform, preening himself in front of a full-length mirror.
0.06½   The tailor adjusts an applique on O'Toole's shoulder.
0.07¼   O'Toole pats himself.
0.10⅓   O'Toole yanks out his sword and poses.
0.16½   O'Toole adjusts his belt.
0.21½   O'Toole adjusts his boot.
0.24½   Start dialogue. End music under dialogue.   etc.

After studying the timing sheet, I decided not to catch any definite cues in this scene, but to write a mock military number, ending it with a chord that could be sustained and then faded out under the dialogue.

After writing the sketch, it looked like this:

5-A   CAPTAIN O'TOOLE

Analyzing this sketch, you will note a duet between a muted trumpet and a bassoon. The background is pizzicato strings. The rhythmic pattern is an imitation of drum beats. As a whole, the music should be a comedy military number.

Since the sketch is very clear orchestrally, the arrangement is not shown.

When I examined the timing sheet of scene 5-B, I found it to be the click track number. The story concerned the two old Irish characters having a fight with two of the thugs—the scene being shot for comedy. The object of the music was to punctuate the blows which were struck and any of the action that could be caught. This sheet was not written in seconds, but the action was described to occur on certain clicks. The click sheet looked like this:

MUSIC 5-B   "THE IRISHMAN"

The Fight

Click 1	Sock on the jaw.
Click 3	Thug yells.
Click 6	Thugs start for door.
Click 8	Mike and Ike grab thug.
Click 11 & 12	They hurl him.
Click 14	He stops rolling.
Click 15	Mike runs after the other thug.
Click 19	Mike hits thug.
Click 21	Thug staggers into chair.
Click 26	Ike hits thug with chair.
Click 27	Cut to thug on floor.
Click 28	The other thug reacts.
Click 29	Thug yells: "Pat!"
Click 31	He yells: "Come on!"
Click 32½	They start for door.
Click 40	Mike hits thug with chair.
Click 42	He gets up and runs.
Click 49½	Ike hits thug on the jaw.
Click 51¼	Mike turns chair over.
Click 54	Picks up club.
Click 55	Throws it.
Click 56½	Club hits thug. etc.

Before starting the sketch of this, I laid out a click sheet on paper in order to see, in written form, the action in relation to the clicks. This was the plan of the click sheet:

With this lay-out you can see the plan more clearly and on just which beat or off-beat the action occurs. There are two clicks in each bar on the accented beats. If some action occurs, as on the 32½ click in this scene, it means that the accent will fall on the eighth note following the 32nd click.

After writing the sketch, it looked like this:

5-B

THE FIGHT

When analyzing this sketch, you will see that a chord accentuates the sock on the jaw. From here on the object is to write something interesting musically, underscoring the action at the same time.

The most satisfactory method of studying this scene is to compare the lay-out sheet (of clicks) with the orchestra sketch. You can then readily see exactly what was written to fit the action.

As this sketch is self-explanatory with regard to the orchestration, the score will not be shown.

I now had completed five reels and was progressing with more speed. I realized that the greater amount of music would be in the last few reels where the action began, but I felt that I would be finished in time.

On studying scene 6-A, I realized that it required two different moods. In the story, O'Toole had gone to see Stanhope whom he had wounded in a duel. In the hallway he met Maureen, who treated him rather severely. Finally she told O'Toole that he had wounded the man whom she was planning to marry. This was rather a shock and a disappointment to O'Toole. In his gracious way he told her that he would continue to be her friend and fight beside Stanhope.

The timing sheet of scene 6-A read:

MUSIC 6-A   "THE IRISHMAN"

The Man I Marry

0.00	Music starts after O'Toole's line: "I'm sorry."
0.01½	The look on his face denotes disappointment.
0.03½	Slowly Maureen lowers her head.
0.08½	She says: "I, too."
0.09⅓	O'Toole walks toward Maureen.
(0.12)	Maureen starts to turn.
0.14½	She says: "Forgive me. I had to strike back."
(0.17¼)	Maureen looks up at O'Toole and says: "Phillip told me how it happened."
(0.21¼)	She pleads with him to be her friend and continue to help her cause.

(1.02⅓) Fade full out. Start to fade in on countryside, O'Toole walking by a blockade.

(1.05) Fade in on L.S. of O'Toole pacing back and forth.

1.12   Dialogue starts with companion. End music.

After studying the timing sheet, I planned to open the scene after O'Toole's line, "I'm sorry," with a passage played by the celli and violas, muted. It should have a feeling of disappointment. The tempo should be slow enough to give the music an opportunity to create this emotional feeling; five seconds a bar would be right.

At twelve seconds (0.12), I would have to create a slight feeling of tragedy as Maureen realized that she had hurt his feelings and that a union between them was impossible. As two bars at five seconds would total ten seconds, I would have to write one 2/4 bar to arrive at twelve seconds.

At seventeen and one-fourth seconds (0.17¼), she softened her speech, and at twenty-one and one-fourth seconds (0.21¼) she started her plea for O'Toole to be her friend. Under this dialogue, beginning at twenty-one and one-fourth seconds (0.21¼), I planned to employ the love theme in a slightly different manner.

When I finished the sketch, it looked like this:

6-A

THE MAN I MARRY

In the analysis of this sketch you will notice the passage
that was written for the celli and violas. At bar 4, the C chord
puts more emphasis on the break between them. At fourteen
and one-half seconds (0.14½) Maureen says, "I had to strike
back." This is two seconds after the C chord is struck. An
English horn enters, creating a feeling of remorse.

At seventeen and one-fourth seconds (0.17¼) when she
softens, the chord construction is planned so that it will not
only lead into bar 7, but will also create a more pleasant feeling
between the characters.

At twenty-one and one-fourth seconds (0.21¼) the love
melody starts. The treatment is not of the lilting character in
which it has been presented previously, but in a slower tempo
to create a more unhappy mood, for although O'Toole is gracious and friendly, he is unhappy because the girl he loves
is going to marry someone else. Notice that the melody is
written in 4/4 time. Previously it had been written:

but now it is written:

At one minute, two and one-third seconds (1.02⅓), the
picture fades into the countryside. At one minute and five
seconds (1.05), a diminished chord gives a slightly ominous
feeling. The English horn plays the principal theme as O'Toole
paces back and forth.

The following is the orchestra score of scene 6-A:

THE MAN I MARRY

6-A

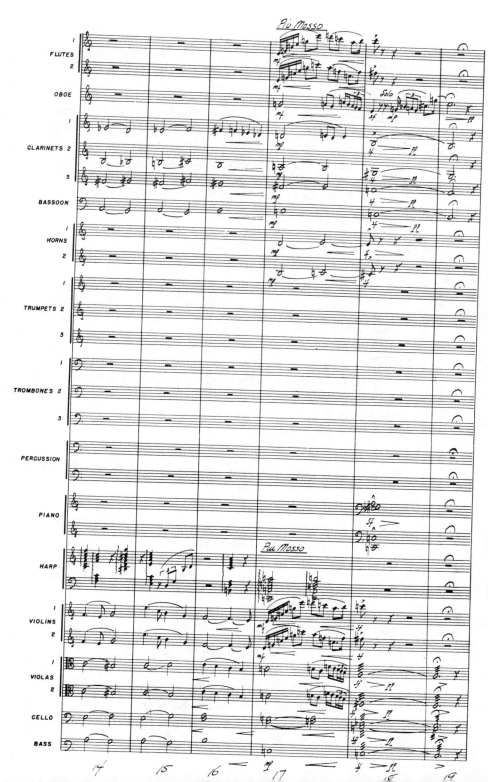

When I looked over scene 6-B, I saw that I had to contend with Kitty again. In the story, Stanhope was carrying on a clandestine affair with her, although he was engaged to marry Maureen. They were at a small cottage when Maureen arrived unexpectedly. Stanhope hid Kitty, but Maureen discovered her. Then Stanhope told Maureen that O'Toole was in love with Kitty and had hidden her in the cottage.

The timing sheet read:

MUSIC 6-B   "THE IRISHMAN"

Kitty

0.00   Music starts as we dissolve to L.S. of the cottage where Stanhope and Kitty are.

0.02   Diss. full in.

0.03⅔   Middle of diss. to Kitty and Stanhope.

(0.05)   Diss. full in. Kitty and Stanhope are seated across the table from each other, playing a game with twine.

0.06⅔   O.S. we hear a knock on the door.

0.07⅔   Stanhope says: "Come in."

0.09   Cut to M.S.—a soldier enters.

0.11   Kitty and Stanhope continue to play. Stanhope says: "What is it?"

0.13   The soldier says: "A carriage is coming."

0.14⅔   Stanhope says: "Good; perhaps it's Hendrigg."

0.18⅔   Pause. He looks at Kitty.

0.19⅔   He goes to the window.

(0.26⅓) Cut to L.S.—We see a carriage crossing the bridge.

(0.29⅔) Cut to interior of cottage. Stanhope turns to Kitty and says: "Quickly, get in there." Points to a room.

(0.31⅔) Cut to M.S. Ext. of the cottage.

0.35   We see Maureen step out of the carriage.

(0.38⅓) Cut to M.S. Int. of cottage. Stanhope closes the door of the room where Kitty is.

0.39⅔   He starts to straighten up the room and puts on his coat.

(0.48)   Cut to C.S., shooting toward the front door, as Maureen enters.

0.49⅓   Maureen steps past the soldier as he says: "Lady Maureen." End music on a sustained chord.

After studying the timing sheet, I decided to open on the long shot with a sort of a pastorale.

At five seconds (0.05), the picture dissolved to the interior of the cottage where the game with the string was in progress. Thinking that it would be an excellent idea to catch the action closely, I called the music cutter and said, "Check scene 6-B again in the moviola. If I remember correctly, this string game was something like pattycake. I would like to know how many times they lean over and touch their hands together."

"Okay," he replied. "I'll check on it and call you back."

He had the information in a short while: "They lean over and touch hands nine times."

"Good," I said. "I'll try to catch those pats in the music, and by watching the screen closely I think I can match the action when I conduct the music."

I hung up and went back to the sketch. At five seconds (0.05) I would start a rocking movement, using Kitty's theme.

After writing it, the sketch looked like this:

In the analysis of this sketch you can see a pastorale opening over the exterior long shot.

At five seconds (0.05), the down-beat of the bar represents the pat of the hands. A wood-wind glissando effect, with a violin trill, accompanies the action of Kitty and Stanhope as they lean back from the pat of their hands.

At twenty-six and one-third seconds (0.26⅓), the picture cuts to a long shot of the carriage crossing the bridge. These two bars have a distinct change of key.

At twenty-nine and two-thirds seconds (0.29⅔), the music resolves to a dramatic chord which will also give a feeling of suspense when the picture cuts inside the cottage as Stanhope tries to rush Kitty into the other room.

I continued with the sketch in this suspensive vein until I had reached thirty-eight and one-third seconds (0.38⅓). Here the picture cut back inside where Stanhope was rushing around trying to straighten up the room. At this point I should have an agitato.

The sketch from thirty-eight and one-third seconds (0.38⅓) on read:

6-B   KITTY (Cont'd.)

You will observe here that an agitato is created by the strings. A wood-wind figuration runs throughout, adding to the excitement. This should be played softly.

At forty-eight seconds (0.48), when the front door opens, it resolves to a chord, which is sustained for an effect of suspense. This is faded out under the dialogue.

Following are the orchestra scores of 6-B and 6-B continued:

6-B   **KITTY**

FLUTES 1 2
OBOE
CLARINETS 1 2 3
BASSOON
HORNS 1 2
TRUMPETS 1 2 3
TROMBONES 1 2 3
PERCUSSION
PIANO
HARP
VIOLINS 1 2
VIOLAS 1 2
CELLO
BASS
8 9 10 11 12 13 14 15 16

6-B

KITTY (Cont'd.)

The timing sheet of scene 6-C revealed that some action was beginning to develop and also that the relationship between Maureen and O'Toole was becoming strained because she had been told by Stanhope that Kitty was O'Toole's girl friend.

The timing sheet read:

MUSIC 6-C   "THE IRISHMAN"
                   Take Your Places

0.00   Music starts on M.S., O'Toole and his men at a campfire, after his line: "Come on, men, take your places."
0.02   Cut to M.L.S., Maureen's carriage approaching.
(0.04⅔)   Cut to M.S., O'Toole steps forward.
(0.07)   Cut to C.U. of Maureen inside the carriage.
0.09⅔   O.S. we hear O'Toole say, "Good evening."
0.11½   Maureen looks away.
(0.14⅓)   Camera holds on 2 S., O'Toole says: "Thousands of welcomes you'll find here."
0.18⅔   Cut to C.U. of Maureen: "Still a Romeo."
(0.23)   Cut to C.U. of O'Toole as he says: "Yes."
(0.29½)   Cut to 2 S., Maureen says: "Our worlds are far apart—stop these attentions."
0.35   Maureen looks away.
(0.40)   Cut·to O'Toole.
0.43¼   Cut to reverse shot. Maureen says: "Good night."
0.47   Cut to M.S. O'Toole puts on his hat.
0.50⅓   He says: "I'm going to take that castle tonight."
0.52   He·starts to mount his horse.
0.54⅔   Cut to C.U. Maureen says: "How?"
0.56⅔   Cut to M.S. O'Toole mounted on the horse as he says: "We'll meet again."
1.01⅔   Cut to O'Toole. He starts to ride out of the picture.
1.07⅔   O'Toole gallops away. End of music and end of reel.

After studying the timing sheet, I decided to start this scene with a sustained chord in the lower register.

At four and two-thirds seconds O'Toole approached carriage to talk with Maureen, happy to see her and not knowing she was angry with him. I planned to describe this action with a variation of the principal theme. I would try to change moods on each cut from Maureen to O'Toole—the music being rather sullen on her cuts and gay on his.

At forty-four seconds (0.44), I would start a development with the principal theme, which would build into the scene to follow, 6-D.

The sketch I wrote looked like this:

*Analyzing this sketch, you will note the sustained chord
at the beginning for suspense.*

*At four and two-third seconds (0.04⅔), when O'Toole
steps forward, there is a slight movement as the chord changes.*

*At seven seconds (0.07), as O'Toole approaches Maureen,
the principal theme is played by a clarinet.*

*At fourteen and one-third seconds (0.14⅓), as he says,
"Thousands of welcomes you'll find here," there is a sustained
chord that gives a feeling of "What's going to happen now?"*

*At eighteen and two-thirds seconds (0.18⅔), on the cut
to Maureen, the violins and English horn play a phrase that
is rather sullen.*

*At twenty-three seconds (0.23), in the close-up of O'Toole,
the clarinet plays the gay principal theme again.*

*At twenty-nine and one-half seconds (0.29½), on the cut
to Maureen, the character of the music once more becomes
sullen.*

*After Maureen says, "Good night," the wood-winds start
a build on the principal theme that is alternated in the wood-
winds in unison and octaves.*

*To start the excitement as O'Toole mounts his horse, the
strings are tremolo at fifty-two seconds (0.52). The tension
mounts as we approach a chase. At bar 19, the horns enter
with a phrase which will be developed at the beginning of
the next scene.*

I now had six reels finished. The timing sheet of scene
7-A read:

MUSIC 7-A   "THE IRISHMAN"

O'Toole Trapped

0.00	Music starts at the beginning of reel of M.S. of O'Toole's troops.
0.01	O'Toole rides in on his horse.
0.01⅓	He calls out: "All right, lads, cover me when I ride to the castle."
0.04	He gallops out of picture.
(0.05)	Cut to M.S. of the men. One says: "There he goes—to his own funeral."

0.12 Cut to M.L.S. of the road, O'Toole galloping,
      camera left to right.

0.14⅔ O.S., we hear his men firing to cover his ride.

0.16⅓ Cut to M.L.S. shooting toward castle. He rides in.

0.18½ He dismounts and slaps the horse away.

0.21½ He looks toward camera, turns and runs toward
       a drawbridge.   etc.

As I started to write this scene, I realized that I would
have to continue from where I had stopped at the end of Reel
VI, which was:

I decided to start scene 7-A like this:

*The changes of chord from an F flat major seventh to
F minor, and the horn phrase being raised one-half tone, give
the piece a lift.*

At five seconds (0.05), as there was a piece of dialogue,
I would write the music so that it would not interfere by being
too heavy.

At twelve seconds (0.12), I would continue the excitement.

After writing the sketch, it looked like this:

O'TOOLE TRAPPED

7-A

Analyzing this sketch, you will notice that the horn passage is continued.

At bars 5 and 6, the full orchestra plays up to the downbeat of bar 7, which is accented.

As the picture cuts to O'Toole's men with a piece of dialogue, only the basses are sustained. There is also a tempo change "Meno" under this scene, but at twelve seconds (0.12), the action resumes as O'Toole gallops along the road, with the music returning "A tempo."

At eighteen and one-half seconds (0.18½), he dismounts from his horse, so this low trill gives a suspense to the action as he looks toward the castle.

At twenty-one and one-half seconds (0.21½), the music of action and suspense continues as O'Toole tricks the guards into letting him enter the castle.

Following is the orchestra score of scene 7-A:

O'TOOLE TRAPPED

7-A

ALLEGRO
1
FLUTES
2
OBOE
1
CLARINETS 2
3
BASSOON
1
HORNS
2
1
TRUMPETS 2
3
1
TROMBONES 2
3
PERCUSSION
PIANO
HARP
1
VIOLINS
2
1
VIOLAS
2
CELLO
BASS
9
10
11
12
13
14

The next scene to be written was the dream sequence. As O'Toole entered the castle in the preceding scene, the picture cut to Maureen asleep in her room. She tossed about restlessly. With a trick dissolve we were into a scene portraying her dream. In it she saw O'Toole being tortured and, realizing that she was in love with him, she cried out for them to stop.

The timing sheet read:

MUSIC 7-B　　　　　"THE IRISHMAN"
The Dream

0.00　Music starts on trick dissolve.
(0.03)　Diss. full in to O'Toole, in chains, being led in.
(0.07)　Maureen is standing at a window—she tries to cry out to him.
0.11　He is led to a torture block.
0.15　He is placed on it. There is a wheel that they will turn to torture him.
0.19　Maureen cries out in anguish.
(0.24)　They turn the wheel. O'Toole's face shows pain. Maureen is still crying out.
0.26　They turn again.
0.28　They turn again.
0.30　They turn again.
0.32　They turn again.
0.35　Maureen screams.
0.38　Start to dissolve.
0.42　Dissolve full out to Maureen asleep.

After studying the timing sheet, I decided to write an eerie effect over the dissolve. When the picture dissolved into the scene where O'Toole was being led in, I would create an ominous sound in the lower register.

When Maureen cried out (in this dream there would be no sound), I could create an effect of anguish in two ways: the celli on a phrase to be recorded separately and then put through the echo chamber in the final dubbing for a weird effect, or by using women's voices on a phrase in the upper register to be put through the echo and reverberation chamber. The women's voices, especially sopranos, written high and hummed, sound weird when treated in this manner.

The machines that carry the reels of dialogue —
sound effects and music.

For the dream scene in this picture, I decided to use the celli effect. As the budget was set, bringing in voices would entail an extra expenditure.

When I wrote the sketch, it looked like this:

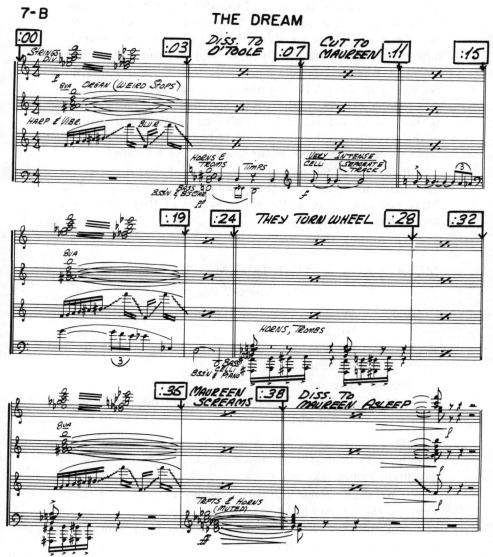

The string trills, the organ, the harp, and the vibraphone furnish the weird effect here. The "vib blurr" means to leave the damper off and run scales up and down making the blurr.

At three seconds (0.03), the low trombones and horns play a soft, menacing chord. The celli furnish the emotion when Maureen tries to cry out. Violas could be added to this to end at bar 6. It goes out of range in bar 6. When they turn the wheel, the chords and heavy bass runs describe the torture.

The dream scene completed Reel VII so I turned to the beginning of Reel VIII. At this point in the story, O'Toole was held a captive in the castle and had been sentenced to be shot. Mike and Ike heard of this and rushed to the scene of the execution so that they could bribe the firing squad. They were successful in their mission, and O'Toole escaped.

Referring to the timing sheet, I noticed that the scene to be underscored was very short—only eight seconds—showing Mike and Ike riding to the castle as fast as they could in a cart pulled by a donkey.

The timing sheet read:

MUSIC 8-A   "THE IRISHMAN"

To Save O'Toole

0.00   Music begins as we start to dissolve to Mike and Ike in the cart.

0.02⅔   Dissolve in. Mike and Ike riding rapidly down the road.

0.06⅔   Start to dissolve.

0.08   Middle of dissolve to M.L.S. of the castle. Segue to 8-B, drums.

This scene segued into a drum track. The firing squad, marching to drums, was proceeding to the yard where the execution would take place.

This drum track is made separately to a click-tempo track in the tempo of the marching.

The music of scene 8-A should be of a humorous nature so I wrote the sketch thus:

8-A   TO SAVE O'TOOLE

In the analysis of this sketch you will notice a descending pattern in the violins and wood-winds, while the brass has an ascending pattern.

At bar 5, the trumpets start a rollicking phrase, answered by the trombones and embellished by a trilling effect in the strings and wood-winds.

The following is **the orchestra score** of scene 8-A:

TO SAVE O'TOOLE

8-A

As the story continued, a fleet of enemy ships arrived off the coast and were awaiting Hendrigg's arrival to explain the plan of attack. I examined scene 8-B and found that it was a cut to the coast with Hendrigg looking for the ships.

The timing sheet read:

MUSIC 8-B   "THE IRISHMAN"
                      The Fleet

0.00   Music starts as we dissolve to Hendrigg at the shore.
0.01⅓   Dissolve full in. He is looking out to sea with a spy-glass.
0.04⅓   He says: "It's them, all right."
0.07⅓   He says: "We can go now."
0.08⅔   They prepare to get into a rowboat.
(0.12½)   Middle of dissolve to three ships.
0.14   Dissolve full in.
(0.18½)   Dissolve to the deck of the flagship.
0.19½   Hendrigg says to the Admiral: "We will signal when all is clear."
0.24½   The Admiral says: "How?"
0.27   Hendrigg says: "One flare if the coast is clear."
0.29½   The Admiral says: "What if you fail?"
0.35   Hendrigg says: "We'll send two flares then."
(0.39)   Hendrigg shakes hands and exits.
0.41⅓   Fade out. End of music.

After studying the timing sheet, I decided to open the scene with the menace theme as Hendrigg was looking for the ships.

At twelve and one-half seconds (0.12½), when the picture dissolved to the ships, I would write a brass passage, maybe something that had a military feeling, but with a rather ominous sound.

At eighteen and one-half seconds (0.18½), I would write for suspense under the dialogue between Hendrigg and the Admiral.

At thirty-nine seconds (0.39), as Hendrigg left the ship, I would write something ominous.

When I completed the sketch, it looked like this:

8-B

THE FLEET

You will see, in the analysis of this sketch, that it begins with the menace theme.

At twelve and one-half seconds (0.12½), where we see the ships, the trumpets and horns play a military phrase. The trombones play a C minor chord in bar 4, and the bass moves up to an A flat in bar 5, making the chord an A flat major seventh chord, which resolves on the last beat to an A flat seventh chord at eighteen and one-half seconds (0.18½). The minor chord construction gives the music an ominous sound.

At eighteen and one-half seconds (0.18½), the A flat chord in the strings has a dramatic effect, tremolo. These chords progress every few bars, through which a horn passage is played. This should dub under the dialogue satisfactorily.

At thirty-nine seconds (0.39), when Hendrigg exits, the full orchestra plays an ominous phrase.

The following is the orchestra score of scene 8-B:

8-B

THE FLEET

In the meantime, while Hendrigg had been on the ship, O'Toole had escaped and made his way back to Maureen. While she was having dinner in the garden with her father and Stanhope, O'Toole slipped over the wall in the dark and hid. Maureen, thinking O'Toole had been executed, was very sad and finally left the table to walk through the garden. O'Toole, from his hiding place, attracted her attention.

The timing sheet for this scene, 8-C, read:

MUSIC 8-C   "THE IRISHMAN"

Surprised

0.00	Music starts as Maureen rises from the table.
0.02⅓	Her father stands up.
0.07⅔	Maureen starts to walk away from the table.
(0.13½)	She starts into the garden.
0.18	O.S., we hear her father and Stanhope talking.
(0.23)	Cut to C.U. of O'Toole's face framed through the bushes.
(0.27)	Maureen walking toward camera.
0.31⅓	She stops, starts to raise her handkerchief to her face.
(0.35⅔)	O.S. we hear O'Toole whisper to Maureen.
(0.38)	She looks up.
0.39	He talks to her.
(0.42)	She says: "O'Toole."
0.42⅔	Dialogue starts in whispered tones.
0.54⅔	Her eyes betray her feeling for him.
(1.07)	O.S. We hear her father say: "Maureen."

After studying the timing sheet, I decided to start this scene with a celli passage, as Maureen's emotions were those of sadness.

At thirteen and one-half seconds (0.13½), as she started toward the garden, the music should be emotionally intense.

At twenty-three seconds (0.23), when O'Toole's face was seen, we could employ a light phrase played by a wood-wind to keep the music in his carefree character.

At twenty-seven seconds (0.27), as Maureen walked along, the music should be something which described her feeling—

sorrow, depression, anguish or remorse.

At thirty-five seconds (0.35), when O'Toole whispered, the music should be hesitant.

At thirty-eight seconds (0.38), when she looked up, the music should have a dramatic or a surprised effect.

At forty-two seconds (0.42), when she realized that it was O'Toole, alive, the music should describe contentment.

At one minute and seven seconds (1.07), when we heard her father call, the music should have an interruption of mood—something to remind her that she had to return to a situation which she did not relish.

After writing the sketch, it looked like this:

8-C   SURPRISED

Analyzing this sketch, you will note many changes of mood.

At the opening when Maureen rises from the table think-ing O'Toole is dead, she is very remorseful because now she realizes that she loved him. To create this feeling in the music, the celli, reinforced with a bass clarinet, play a motif that describes her feelings reaching a low ebb, especially in bar 2 where the music continues to descend to the B in bar 3. This is also made more emphatic by being in minor.

When she starts for the garden at thirteen and one-half seconds (0.13½), the violins and violas join the celli. The dynamics, crescendo, with all the strings in unison, will give a highly emotional effect.

At twenty-three seconds (0.23), when we see O'Toole's face, there is a distinct change of mood. The color of the wood-winds here is in keeping with his character—light and rather gay.

At twenty-seven seconds (0.27), when we see Maureen walking, the strings enter again. In bar 9, the dotted sixteenths and descending harmony describe her emotional feelings of remorse.

When O'Toole whispers at thirty-five and two-thirds seconds (0.35⅔), we have reached a sustained chord or hesi-tation. When recording, it is better to reach this chord at thirty-five seconds (0.35), before he whispers his line. This method is more effective, and the music will not interfere with the soft line he whispers. The ¾ bar is written here to adjust the timing for the important cue at thirty-eight seconds (0.38). Here the wood-winds and the horns interrupt the mood with a dramatic or a surprised movement as Maureen hears O'Toole's voice.

At forty-two seconds (0.42), when she realizes that O'Toole is alive, a placid melody enters to describe her relief and contentment. This continues until the time her father calls her at one minute and seven seconds (1.07). The surprise chord here at bar 18 describes the interruption of her happy mood.

The following is the orchestra score of scene 8-C:

SURPRISED

8-C

I was now nearing the end of Reel VIII, and the next two short scenes would finish it.

In the progression of the story, O'Toole wanted to expose Stanhope as a traitor. O'Toole slipped into Stanhope's room to find a letter, and while he was there Stanhope came in and discovered him. O'Toole made his escape through the door, climbed down a trellis, and hid as the guards looked for him.

The timing sheet of scene 8-D read:

MUSIC 8-D   "THE IRISHMAN"
                         Discovered

0.00   Music starts as O'Toole hears a noise O.S.
0.02   He looks for a place to hide.
0.04⅔   He starts to run toward the door.
0.09   He is hiding behind the door as Stanhope starts to enter the room.
0.12   Stanhope closes the door and looks around.
0.15   He walks across the room opposite the door.
0.19⅔   O'Toole starts to run from behind the door. Stanhope draws his gun. End music. Segue to 8-E.

After studying the timing sheet, I decided to write a movement of suspense that would be an agitato. When I wrote the sketch, it looked like this:

Analyzing this sketch, the C tremolo in the violins creates the suspense. The celli and bass clarinet with the bassoon give the agitato effect. The wood-wind chords starting at bar 7 are dark in color and add to the suspense.

This scene is an overlap; that is, the last chord of the outgoing track and the first chord of the incoming track are struck together. Therefore, I finished this scene, 8-D, on the down-beat of bar 11, or at nineteen and two-thirds seconds (0.19 2/3) with an F minor chord. As this last chord would *be hit simultaneously with the opening chord of the next scene, 8-E, in the final dubbing, both of these would have to be F minor chords.*

Examining the timing sheet of scene 8-E, I found it to read:

MUSIC 8-E   "THE IRISHMAN"

Escape

0.00	Music starts as O'Toole rushes for the door.
(0.01½)	As he pulls the door shut, Stanhope fires.
0.02⅓	The door slams. Stanhope runs toward it.
0.04⅔	Stanhope opens the door and runs into the hall.
(0.07)	He yells: "Guard! Guard!"
0.08	He yells: "It's O'Toole—get after him!"
0.10⅔	The guards run to catch O'Toole.
0.14¼	Cut to another section of the hall.
0.17¼	Cut to C.U. of Stanhope: "Shoot to kill!"
0.19½	End of music. End of reel.

When I studied the timing sheet, I realized that here I had a change-over problem because, coming at the end of Reel VIII, this would be a mechanical switch of the projection equipment in the theatres. This was particularly awkward as a chase had just begun.

At the opening of this scene, I would have to start in F minor (the chord which finished scene 8-D) and would have to create much excitement as O'Toole ran for the door.

At seven seconds (0.07), when Stanhope yelled, "Guard!" I would diminish down to a soft, dramatic scherzo.

Before nineteen and one-half seconds (0.19½), I planned to arrive at a sustained note, probably trilled. With this device I could start Reel IX with the same note so that the change-over would not be apparent in the theatre.

When I wrote the sketch, it looked like this:

8-E

ESCAPE

The analysis of this sketch reveals the exciting movement in the strings as O'Toole runs toward the door. The horns play an accented F minor chord. The effect here will be a crescendo, the climax occurring at bar 3, with the full orchestra.

The strings and wood-winds then continue with a phrase of the principal theme. A descending scale continues to bar 8, where a modulating chord leads into the soft, dramatic scherzo at bar 9 or seven seconds (0.07) in the key of E minor. This proceeds to bar 23, where the movement stops, but to maintain the excitement the sustained note is trilled.

As I prepared to start scene 9-A, I kept in mind that I would have to begin it with a B natural trill. The timing sheet read:

MUSIC 9-A   "THE IRISHMAN"
                          The Hunted

0.00	Music starts at beginning of reel as the guards are still looking for O'Toole.
0.06	Cut to garden. O'Toole drops to the ground from trellis.
(0.07⅓)	He lands on the ground, stands for a moment looking around.
0.08	He starts to run.
0.10	He stops and looks around.
0.13⅔	Cut to C.U. of O'Toole as he slips into the bushes near a window.
0.16⅔	Cut to M.S. as some guards walk into the garden.
0.19	Cut to C.U. of O'Toole watching the guards.
0.23	Some guards run into picture camera right and out camera left.

After studying the timing sheet, I assumed that the trill would be all right for the action at this point since the guards were merely looking around the hall. The trilled note would also be good for suspense.

When O'Toole landed on the ground at seven and one-third seconds (0.07⅓), this would be the perfect place to resume the scherzo. As this scene should have a feeling of agitato behind his attempt to elude the guards, the scherzo would be excellent throughout his escape.

When I wrote the sketch, it looked like this:

9-A   **THE HUNTED**

*In analyzing this sketch you will see the B natural trill
at the beginning. To this has been added a horn passage which*

is, in reality, a continuation of the horn passage at the end of scene 8-E.

When O'Toole lands on the ground at seven and one-third seconds (0.07⅓), the scherzo resumes. On the downbeat of bar 9, where he hits the ground, an accented chord points up this action. The violins expound the theme of the scherzo and are answered in imitation by the basses and celli.

The scene continued in this vein as O'Toole climbed back up the trellis and hid in the room, trying to see Maureen.

Examining scene 9-B, I saw that it was one between Maureen and O'Toole. He was hiding in the room, but stepped out to meet her as she entered. At this time she thought he was a traitor, being convinced of this by Stanhope, who had made the accusation to cover up his own guilt.

The timing sheet read:

MUSIC 9-B   "THE IRISHMAN"

At Last

Establishing shot: O'Toole is hidden in the room. In the adjoining room, Stanhope and Maureen's father have been telling her that O'Toole is a traitor.

0.00	Music starts in room where O'Toole is hiding as Maureen enters after having just left her father.
0.02⅔	She shuts door and locks it.
(0.05)	She walks hurriedly camera left.
0.09	She reaches another door and starts to open it.
0.11	She steps through the door.
0.13	She comes back.
(0.16)	The curtain begins to move and we start to see O'Toole.
0.16⅔	Cut to C.U. of O'Toole.
0.20	Maureen says: "For heaven's sake, leave here!"
0.23	He looks out of the window.
0.24⅔	He takes her by the hand and says: "Come with me."
0.25⅔	She says: "You are quite mad."
0.28⅔	She says: "I'm not going to marry you—a traitor."
0.30⅔	Cut to shot favoring O'Toole. He says: "I think

you love me."

(0.34)   Cut to Maureen as she says: "No, you had better go."

0.38   He takes her in his arms and tells her he loves her.

After studying the timing, I decided to open this scene
with a mood of sadness as Maureen entered the room. Although
she had been told O'Toole was a traitor, she believed she loved
him. As she walked quickly across the room, the music should
have a feeling of agitato—she is bewildered.

When the curtain parted to begin to reveal O'Toole, the
mood should change to something a little brighter. Then at
twenty seconds (0.20) when she said, "For heaven's sake, leave
here," there should be a pleading phrase in the music.

At twenty-eight and two-thirds seconds (0.28⅔), after
she told him she was not going to marry him, there should be
something to describe that mood.

After writing the sketch, it looked like this:

*In the analysis of this sketch you notice a string passage
that denotes a little unhappiness as Maureen enters the room.
When she walks quickly to the other door at five seconds
(0.05), the violins start a tremolo passage which is answered
by the celli.*

*When we see O'Toole at sixteen seconds (0.16), the mood
changes to a lighter character.*

*After Maureen's line ending, ". . . leave here," there is a
pleading phrase in the violins.*

*At twenty-eight seconds (0.28), where she says she is not
going to marry him, the harmonic construction descends, ex-
pressing a slight unhappiness.*

*At thirty-eight seconds (0.38), where he takes her in his
arms, the love theme begins (but is not shown).*

The love theme continued (subsequent to the material
shown in the sketch) throughout the complete scene as they
confessed their love for each other. It ended at two minutes and
eighteen and one-third seconds (2.18⅓), as O'Toole left Maureen, promising to come back after he was cleared of treason.
Actually he was waiting for an opportunity to unmask Stanhope.

When I examined scene 9-C, I saw that it was the one in
which Stanhope was exposed. O'Toole had burst into the room
where Maureen, her father and Stanhope were conversing. He
accused Stanhope and tried to pull a letter from Stanhope's
coat which would give him away. Hendrigg entered at this
point and held a gun on them while Stanhope left. Then Kitty
entered the room and assisted O'Toole in escaping so that he
could stop Stanhope.

The timing sheet read:

MUSIC 9-C   "THE IRISHMAN"
                   Stanhope Unmasked

0.00   Music starts as O'Toole grabs Stanhope's coat
           for letter.

0.03⅔   Cut to Hendrigg at the door with two guns.

0.07   He tells Stanhope to leave.

(0.20⅔)   Cut to M.S. O'Toole starts to step forward. Hen-
           drigg raises his guns.

0.25   Hendrigg starts to close the door.

0.31   O.S. we hear a knock.

0.32⅓   As the door starts to open, camera begins to pan.

0.33½   As he steps back behind the door, we see Kitty.

0.34⅓   She says: "I was trying to find my way out of here."

0.40   As Hendrigg steps out she continues: "I thought the trouble was over."

0.42⅔   Hendrigg replies: "It is."

0.43⅔   Cut to exterior. Stanhope mounts his horse.

0.46⅔   Cut back—Kitty steps forward.

0.47¼   She speaks: "Did Stanhope tell you where he was going?"

(0.49)   O'Toole replies: "No."

0.53¼   O'Toole's head is cocked to one side, hoping she will tell him.

1.03   He looks at Hendrigg, waiting for a chance to make a break.

(1.13⅔)   Kitty steps forward as Hendrigg orders her to close the curtain.

1.15⅔   She glances at the guns and starts to circle Hendrigg.

1.24⅔   The camera moves with Kitty.

1.30⅔   Cut to C.U. of O'Toole, watching.

1.33⅓   Cut to M.S.—Kitty screams and pulls curtain.

1.34⅔   She throws curtain around Hendrigg.

1.36   Hendrigg's gun goes off. End music. Segue to 9-D.

This was a direct segue again—from scene 9-C to 9-D. We had decided to break this at the gun shot and start scene 9-D with the shot.

After studying the timing sheet, I decided to start 9-C with an accented chord to emphasize the drama as O'Toole grabbed Stanhope's coat. I would also use the menace theme under Hendrigg's actions.

At twenty and two-thirds seconds (0.20⅔), I would have another accent as Hendrigg raised his guns.

At forty-three and two-thirds seconds (0.43⅔), on the cut

outside where Stanhope mounted his horse, I would write a more powerful phrase.

At forty-nine seconds (0.49), as O'Toole replied, "No," I would start an agitato to continue up to the point where Kitty threw the curtain. Then I would sustain a chord with a crescendo to lead into scene 9-D where I would accent the shot.

When I wrote the sketch, it looked like this:

9-C

STANHOPE UNMASKED

As you begin to analyze this sketch, you will see the accented chord sustained with the strings tremolo. At bar 2, the menace theme starts as the tremolo continues. This will add more suspense to the drama taking place on the screen.

As O'Toole steps forward and Hendrigg raises his guns, there is a new accent. The wood-winds add suspense at this point.

On the cut to the exterior where Stanhope mounts his horse, trombones are added to the wood-winds to give more power and menace to this section. At bar 12, there is a diminuendo as the picture cuts back to the room.

At forty-nine seconds (0.49), the agitato starts as O'Toole says, "No," and continues to the gun shot.

There is a fresh accent at one minute, thirteen and two-thirds seconds (1.13⅔) where Kitty steps forward to close the curtains.

In the last bar, the music has reached an anticlimax, reinforced by the trombones. A crescendo will lead up to the shot.

Following is the orchestra score of scene 9-C:

9-C   STANHOPE UNMASKED

When I started working on scene 9-D, I knew that it would start with the gun shot. Immediately following it, O'Toole ran and jumped through the window—and the chase was on.

The timing sheet read:

MUSIC 9-D   "THE IRISHMAN"

The Chase

0.00	Music begins as the gun goes off.
0.00⅔	O'Toole starts to run.
(0.02)	O'Toole hits the window, Hendrigg fires.
0.03⅓	Cut to the garden. O'Toole lowers himself to the wall.
0.05⅔	He starts to run along the wall.
0.07½	Cut back to the room—the soldiers rush toward Hendrigg.
0.08½	They grab him.
0.15¼	Cut to exterior. O'Toole running along the wall, camera right to left.
0.16⅔	He starts to jump.
0.17⅓	He lands and continues to run.
0.21	Cut to M.S.—we see a horse standing in front of the gate.
0.25⅓	He stops running.
0.27⅓	He starts to jump.
0.28	He hits the saddle.
(0.29½)	He starts to gallop away. etc.

After studying the timing sheet, I decided to start the music (on the gun shot) with an accented chord.

At two seconds (0.02) there should be an accent as he hits the window.

From this point on, the action consisted of general excitement and a chase up to the cue at twenty-nine and one-half seconds (0.29½). I intended to catch this action with a fresh start in the music.

After writing the sketch, it looked like this:

THE CHASE

Analyzing this sketch, you will notice that the brass has an accented chord at the beginning. The reason for starting on an F minor chord is that the preceding scene, 9-C, ended so that we could segue into scene 9-D on the gun shot.

In other words, the final three bars of scene 9-C and the first bar of scene 9-D look like this:

The ascending harmony in the upper voices and the descending bass give the piece a lift as the new action starts.

After the gun shot, there is a trill that gives suspense until O'Toole hits the window. A brass passage starts here and creates excitement up to the point where he commences running along the wall at five and two-thirds seconds (0.05 ⅔). The strings, wood-winds and horns continue the excitement until we see the horse. Here a variation of the principal theme starts in a minor key.

At twenty-eight seconds (0.28), O'Toole hits the saddle so the music is accented for this in bar 17. The agitation is also relaxed here in preparation for a new beginning of the chase at twenty-nine and one-third seconds (0.29 ⅓).

I continued this scene in this vein—the chase—to the end of it, occurring at one minute and thirty-seven seconds (1.37). This was also the end of the reel.

I now had nine reels finished, and as I examined scene 10-A, I realized that I was nearing the end. As the story continued, the cavalry rode out to help O'Toole, who was still riding in pursuit of Stanhope. Stanhope arrived at the castle ahead of O'Toole, rode over the drawbridge and then ordered it raised so that no one else could enter the castle. O'Toole rode up just in time to jump onto the drawbridge as it was being raised.

The timing sheet read:

MUSIC 10-A   "THE IRISHMAN"

The Cavalry

0.00   Music starts on M.L.S. — the cavalry riding through gates to the rescue.

0.03   Middle of dissolve to castle.

(0.05) Dissolve full in. Stanhope riding across drawbridge.

0.09   He dismounts as we cut to C.S.

0.10⅔   He says: "Raise the drawbridge."

0.12⅔   Stanhope exits.

0.16   Three soldiers run out, camera pans with them.

0.19½   Camera holds on M.S., as they start to raise bridge.

(0.21½) Cut to M.S. O'Toole rides in.

0.23   He swings down from his horse.

0.26⅔   He picks up a shillelagh.

0.27½   He starts toward castle.

0.29½   He sees drawbridge being raised and runs for it.

etc.

After studying the timing sheet, I decided to start with a military effect as the cavalry rode out.

At five seconds (0.05), when the picture cut to the castle, the music should be something of an agitato, but not loud.

At twenty-one and one-half seconds (0.21½) as O'Toole arrived, perhaps there could be more movement in the music with a touch of Irish character.

After writing the sketch, it looked like this:

10-A

THE CAVALRY

When you analyze this sketch, you will see the military effect at the beginning—a sustained chord in the strings and wood-winds, while the trumpet plays a fanfare.

At five seconds (0.05), when the picture cuts to the castle, the agitato is created by the strings (tremolo) and a bass passage. At bar 9, the horns enter. The repeated notes add to the suspense and give the music a more ominous feeling.

At twenty-one and one-half seconds (0.21½), when O'Toole rides in, there is a key change, and the violins start a more active movement. This continues in the same vein with a gradual crescendo until O'Toole jumps onto the drawbridge. As this action is a climax, it is stressed with a climactic chord.

The balance of the scene was a general chase throughout the castle as Stanhope's men tried to capture O'Toole. It ran for two minutes and six seconds (2.06).

Following is the orchestra score of 10-A:

10-A

THE CAVALRY

FLUTES 1 2
OBOE
CLARINETS 1 2 3
BASSOON
HORNS 1 2
TRUMPETS 1 2 3
TROMBONES 1 2 3
PERCUSSION
PIANO
HARP
VIOLINS 1 2
VIOLAS 1 2
CELLO
BASS
cresc.
8
9
10
11
12
13

When I turned to scene 10-B, I saw that it revealed Ike and Mike hurrying to the rescue in their cart, which was loaded down with as many soldiers as they could get into it. The timing sheet read:

MUSIC 10-B   "THE IRISHMAN"
                     O'Toole's Own

0.00   Music starts on cut to Ike and Mike with their cart loaded with O'Toole's soldiers.

0.02⅔   Cut to C.S. Ike says to Mike: "Are they all here?"

0.04⅔   Mike says: "All here."

0.06⅔   Cut to M.L.S. The donkey going as fast as he can, followed by the cavalry.

0.09⅓   The cavalry goes by them.

0.14¾   Cut to M.S. of O'Toole at the castle. He is hiding on a ledge and below we see the ocean.

0.19   He slips.

0.20½   He grabs.

0.24   Cut to overhead shot as he climbs toward camera.

0.27⅓   Cut to M.S. Stanhope and group on top of the tower. Stanhope looks at his watch   etc.

After studying the timing sheet, I planned to open the scene with something which would be humorous, semi-military and rollicking.

At fourteen and three-fourths seconds (0.14¾), there should be suspense because O'Toole was hiding.

After writing the sketch, it looked like this:

10-B   O'TOOLE'S OWN

In the analysis of this sketch, you will see a rollicking, semi-military phrase played by three trumpets. Added to this are string and wood-wind glissandos. The trumpet phrase is repeated by the trombones starting at bar 5.

At fourteen and three-fourths seconds (0.14¾), when the picture cuts back to the castle, the violins sustain a high tremolo for suspense. At bar 11, the horns, wood-winds and the lower strings play soft, accented chords which start at the time he slips on the wall. At bar 16, when the picture cuts to the tower, the basses enter with a sustained note that leads into the menace theme.

As this sketch is clear orchestrally, no score will be shown.

I continued the scene in the same manner under Stanhope's dialogue. They were getting ready to fire the signal rocket to the ships off-shore. O'Toole finally reached the tower where he played havoc with their plans. As the signal was only one rocket, O'Toole set them all ablaze, giving the wrong signal. The entire scene was one minute and forty-six seconds (1.46) in length and finished with the noise of the rockets.

When I examined scene 10-C, I noticed that the picture cut from the rocket scene to the ships off-shore. When the Admiral saw the signal of more than one rocket, he ordered the ships to sail. Then there was another cut of Ike and Mike, delayed because the weight of the soldiers had raised the donkey off the ground. The timing sheet read:

MUSIC 10-C   "THE IRISHMAN"
Wrong Signal

0.00	Music starts on cut to M.S. the Admiral and his staff on board the ship.
0.03⅔	He says: "Something's gone wrong. Order all ships—full sail."
(0.07)	Cut to Ike and Mike. The cart is tipped backward and the donkey's feet are off the ground.
0.09	One of the men pulls on the donkey's head.
0.10	The donkey's feet touch the ground.
0.12⅔	Cut to another angle as the cart starts forward.
0.15⅓	The donkey starts to kick and continues to move forward.
(0.19)	Cut to O'Toole dueling with Stanhope. etc.

I decided to start the cut of the ships with the menace theme.

At seven seconds (0.07), on the cut to the donkey, I would write something humorous with an Irish flavor.

At nineteen seconds (0.19), when the picture cut back to O'Toole dueling, I would resume with fight music.

After writing the sketch, it looked like this:

Analyzing this sketch, you will see the menace theme at
the beginning.

At seven seconds (0.07), my intention is to create a comedy

*feeling, with rips in the trumpets, heavy beats in the basses
and tympani, and trombone glissandos on the third beat. Over
this the strings and the wood-winds play a sort of Irish jig. The
tempo is fairly fast—four bars in five and one-half seconds.*

*At nineteen seconds, when the picture cuts back to O'Toole,
the excitement of the duel starts.*

I continued in this vein throughout the duel. At one minute and twenty-two seconds (1.22), Stanhope had forced
O'Toole into the wall. He had the better of O'Toole when Ike,
Mike and the soldiers arrived. A soldier raised his gun to shoot,
and he fired the shot at one minute, thirty-three and one-half
seconds (1.33½). It was decided to break the take here on the
gun shot (as was done in one of the preceding scenes) and
start scene 10-D with the shot.

Continuing with one minute, twenty-one and one-half
seconds (1.21½), the timing sheet read:

MUSIC 10-C   "THE IRISHMAN"
                 Wrong Signal (Continued)

1.21½   Stanhope forces O'Toole into the wall.

1.23⅓   Cut to C.S.—shooting past O'Toole at Stanhope
        trying to push O'Toole over the wall.

1.25⅓   Cut to C.S.—O'Toole trying to push Stanhope back.

(1.27¾) Cut to M.S.—shooting towards the tower door as
        O'Toole's soldier steps out, carrying a gun.

(1.30½) Cut to C.S.—shooting toward O'Toole as Stanhope
        tries to force him over the wall.

1.32⅓   Cut to soldier as he raises his gun.

1.33½   He fires.

For the greater part of this scene the music should be exciting as Stanhope was trying to push O'Toole over the wall.
Two cues did appear to be important, however, one at one minute, twenty-seven and three-fourths seconds (1.27¾) when
O'Toole's man arrived, and the other at one minute, thirty and
one-half seconds (1.30½) on the cut to Stanhope as he at-
tempted to push O'Toole over the wall.

After writing the sketch, it looked like this:

10-C   WRONG SIGNAL (Cont'd.)

Analyzing this sketch, you will see that in general it consists of exciting music. At bar 56, when O'Toole's man arrives,
the brass has chords in a major key. At bars 57 and 58, when
Stanhope attempts to push O'Toole over the wall, the brass has
forceful chords in the lower register. The high trill continues
throughout the scene, being held until one minute, thirty-three
and one-half seconds (1.33½) when the gun shot occurs.

On looking over scene 10-D, I saw that after Stanhope was
shot, he staggered and was subdued by O'Toole's men.This
ended the fight, and all the traitors were captured. The timing
sheet read:

MUSIC 10-D   "THE IRISHMAN"
                        Foiled

0.00   Music starts on gun shot.
0.01   Cut to M.S.—Stanhope staggers back.
0.02⅓   O'Toole knocks the sword out of Stanhope's hand.
0.04⅓   Cut to M.S.—as officer steps forward.
0.06⅓   The officer and a man grab Stanhope.
0.07   The officer says: "Take him away."
0.08⅔   Cut to C.S.—O'Toole steps in.
0.10   He reaches inside Stanhope's coat and takes letter.
0.12⅔   He says: "This is what I came for."
0.16⅔   He says: "Take him away."
0.22⅔   Cut to M.S.—shooting toward the door as Ike and Mike appear.
0.31½   Mike stops camera foreground and says: "Did we win?"
0.33   O'Toole says: "Yes."
0.34½   O'Toole smiles weakly.
0.37⅓   He starts to slump forward in a faint.
0.38½   Middle of dissolve. Segue to 10-E.

After studying the timing sheet, I decided to open on the gun shot with a brass chord; this should have a shock effect. Then at two and one-third seconds (.02⅓) there should be another accent as O'Toole knocked the sword from Stanhope. I would also employ the menace theme here, in some different form, to emphasize Stanhope's tragic end.

At twenty-two and two-thirds seconds (0.22⅔) as Mike and Ike arrived, I would change the mood, probably using the principal theme with a slight undercurrent because the situation was still rather dramatic.

After writing the sketch, it looked like this:

10-D   FOILED

In the analysis of this sketch, you will notice the brass chord at the beginning, on the gun shot. This is an altered chord that will give a shock effect. It is rather dissonant, being a G seventh chord including both a major fifth, a lowered fifth, and a minor ninth.

At bar 2, or two and one-third seconds (0.02⅓), this resolves into a C major chord (with strings and wood-winds) which is accented as O'Toole knocks the sword from Stanhope's hand. The chord is repeated and establishes a rhythmic pattern that is continued with muted horns at bar 3. This has an ominous sound.

With the muted horns at bar 3, the violas and clarinet

*play the menace theme. Instead of having a menacing sound
here, however, it has a pathetic or a tragic effect—Stanhope's
efforts have been futile.*

*At twenty-two and two-thirds seconds (0.22⅔), when Ike
and Mike arrive, the oboe enters with the principal theme.
Under this the strings have tremolo chords to keep the feeling
of drama sustained.*

*The tension is relaxed somewhat at thirty and one-third
seconds (0.30⅓), and as O'Toole starts to slump forward there
is a crescendo and a diminuendo which also serves as a modulation to the next cue, 10-E.*

*As this would be a direct segue, I had to plan it in ad-
vance. Glancing ahead to 10-E, I intended to use the love theme
and selected the key of D. Therefore, the present chord for the
ending of 10-D is resolved to an A seventh chord.*

Following is the orchestra score of scene 10-D:

FOILED

10-D

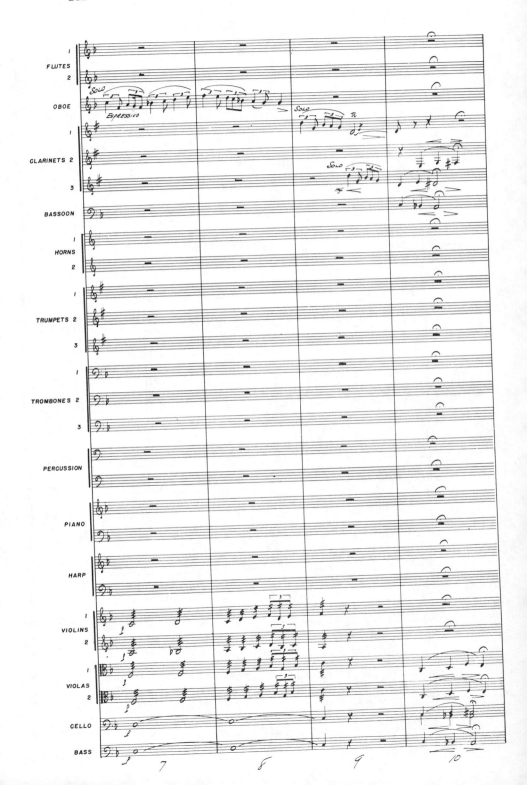

As scene 10-E was a direct segue and I had already decided to employ the love theme, I now had merely to determine the right instrumentation. I referred to the timing sheet which read:

MUSIC 10-E   "THE IRISHMAN"
                    O'Toole Smokes

0.00   Music starts on middle of dissolve to M.L.S. of room of the castle as O'Toole paces the floor smoking his pipe.

0.06   Ike enters with a tray.

0.08   He puts the tray down.

0.15⅔   Ike says: "You're not fooling me."

0.20⅔   He continues: "I know why you're pacing the floor."

0.23   He tells O'Toole that he misses Maureen.

0.29   O'Toole continues to pace.

0.31   Ike continues to talk about Maureen.

0.33⅔   O'Toole starts to walk up the stairs.

0.34⅓   Ike says: "Where are you going?"

0.41   O'Toole says he is going to find her.

0.48   O'Toole finishes speaking and starts to run up the stairs. End of music. Segue to 10-F.

As the general mood of this scene was not too happy, the love melody played by an English horn would be good. O'Toole was thinking of Maureen and felt rather sad that he was not with her. (The key of D was selected because it is a good register for the English horn.)

After writing the sketch, it looked like this:

10-E   O'TOOLE SMOKES

By analyzing this sketch, you can see the English horn solo accompanied by strings. At twenty seconds (0.20) the celli play the melody, with the English horn re-entering in bar 7.

As this sketch is clear orchestrally, no score will be shown.

Examining cue 10-F, I realized I was near the end, since this was the end title. As the story concluded, O'Toole told Ike he was going to look for Maureen. As he started to run up the stairs, he heard Maureen's voice. She had come back to him and asked his forgiveness for believing he had been a traitor.

The timing sheet read:

MUSIC 10-F   "THE IRISHMAN"

End Title

0.00   Music starts as O'Toole turns and starts to run
            up the stairs.
(0.01⅓)   O.S. we hear Maureen speak: "May I come in?"
0.02   O'Toole stops as though shocked.
0.03¼   Cut to C.S.—O'Toole turns and looks.
(0.05⅓)   Cut to M.S.—shooting toward Maureen, who is
            looking very beautiful.
0.07½   Cut to C.S. of O'Toole.
0.08⅔   He says: "Is it really you?"
0.10⅓   He stands looking.
0.10⅔   Cut to Maureen. Slowly she starts to walk toward
            camera.
0.14⅓   She asks him to forgive her.
0.20⅔   She stops walking, camera holds on her. Ike, who
            is standing behind her, exits.
0.21⅔   She asks him if he will have her.
0.24   Cut to O'Toole. He is overjoyed and tells her how
            wonderful it is to be close to her again.
(0.34)   Cut to C.U. of O'Toole smiling.
0.35   He tells her he loves her.
0.40   Cut to C.U.—Maureen as she waits for him.
0.42   Cut to M.S.—shooting past her toward O'Toole.
0.43   He leaps toward her.
(0.45⅔)   They kiss.
0.48⅓   Kiss ends.
0.50⅓   They kiss again as "THE END" starts to appear.
0.57   Fade full out—end of music.

I looked over the timing sheet and realized that I must
start this scene on a chord from the preceding scene 10-E,
which ended in the key of D. It should be something exciting
as he rushed up the stairs.

The first important cue was at five and one-third seconds
(0.05⅓), when the picture cut to Maureen at the doorway.
I would also employ the love theme after they began to talk.

After writing the sketch, it looked like this:

10-F
END TITLE

In analyzing this sketch, you will note that the strings play an ascending scale. This is a D seventh scale to correspond with the ending of the last scene, 10-E, which was in the key of D. This is played very fast and sustains on the note D (fp) as we hear Maureen's off-stage voice.

At five and one-third seconds (0.05⅓) when the picture cuts to Maureen, the strings play a rather sweet phrase; this will have a luscious sound. There is a change of color in bar 5 with the wood-winds. This will give the strings a fresh entrance with the love theme at bar 6.

At thirty-four seconds (0.34), one of the other themes reappears and builds into the kiss at forty-five and two-thirds seconds (0.45⅔)

The last four bars are Irish in character and are played by the full orchestra to the fade out of "THE END."

The following is the orchestra score of the end title:

10-F   **END TITLE**

CHAPTER THREE

STUDENTS' SUMMARY

ON SUMMING up what has been shown in the story (the writing of the music and the arranging), the student can see what the important requirements are:

A. To understand moods in music and to be able to grasp a mood in a pictorial situation. This can be developed by practice. The study of opera scores is very good. Learn the story, go to the opera or listen to records, and hear the dramatic music which has been written to describe a dramatic situation.

In symphonies, you generally have to form your own mental pictures unless a programme note gives you the story which the music is supposed to describe, but in opera there is a definite story for which the music was written.

B. To understand the orchestra. This is a tremendous aid in writing descriptive music. Study the orchestra instruments, their tone colors, and analyze scores while listening to records. Listen to the different moods in different registers, played by the various combinations of orchestral instruments. This is also a very important study for arrangers.

C. To train yourselves to grasp situations fast, to think fast, and to try to get the conception the first time. With the time element involved, there is not much chance to experiment, but don't be too satisfied with what you have done. Try to improve all your work as you go along. You will be able to recognize your mistakes as you progress, both in writing and arranging. Admit them to yourself and make a mental note: "I know what to do *now* if I ever have a similar problem."

D. Be diplomatic. Don't think that every bar of music you
write or arrange is a gem. You may be wrong. If you cannot stand a little criticism, it will be much harder for you
to be successful. Don't forget that someone is paying you to
write music or to arrange. They must be happy with your
work (if you want to do more for them), so be diplomatic
and cooperate with them. If you know they are wrong and
don't understand what is involved, explain it in a nice
manner. Maybe they will see that you are right. Don't
say, "I won't change that."

Moods are sometimes established by association. As an
example, for a street scene (for some reason) everyone seemed
to accept George Gershwin's "An American in Paris" as a pattern. It was imitated so often that almost every time there was
a street scene on the screen, it was a fast two-four piece of
music. His music seems to be associated with a large city, especially New York. In other words, a street is exciting and busy
with taxis, trucks, automobiles, streetcars, etc.

The other type associated with New York is a sophisticated
blues (not the Negro type). I really don't know the explanation
for this, but a precedent must have been established at some
time. In the evolution of jazz music, one strain of the real blues
became a little sophisticated (meaning wise in the ways of the
world—so New York, being the largest city, must be the wisest),
and it became accepted as the theme.

As examples of these two types, we will look at a street
scene:

and a sophisticated blues:

     This theme was used for a New York street scene in
"NAKED CITY." You can see by the chord construction and by
the melody of the number that it has a definite character. In
the picture, this was played during a shot of a deserted street
in New York at night. The melody alone has a melancholy or
lonesome feeling.

     Let us consider the orchestration of this number. The back-
ground should be strings, and the balance would be: the E
played by the first violins; the quarter notes, B and A, played
by the second violins; the F played by the violas; the A played
by the celli; and the D played by the bass. You have several
choices for the melody instrument; it is indicated "Trpt." in the
sketch. Do you know why this is a good choice? We are back to
precedent again—it sounds more "New Yorkish." I don't know
why, but we are used to that sound. A very good color for this
would be an alto flute; the range is good, and it would really
give this a lonesome sound.

     This could be arranged in many ways. Say, for instance,
that the harmony parts are scored for the lower strings and
wood-winds, with the melody written for violins. The sound
and character of the number would be entirely different—it
would then become sentimental. This is not the impression that
you are trying to create, however; you are trying to create a
lonesome, deserted street with no people visible. Do you see the
difference? Strings are sentimental and warm, whereas the
flute or trumpet give it the feeling of a lonesome street. These
points are brought up to illustrate the importance of orchestration. If you write or arrange this type of music, it is very important to know these details.

     The music writer may say to himself, "Oh, I'll leave that
to the arranger." This is wrong because the composer is closer

to the picture than the arranger, and as he writes he is trying to
create a mood. Where does he create that mood? In the orchestra! (The music itself, of course, must be of the correct mood,
but the orchestra interprets it.)

The arranger may say to himself, "I wonder what he
meant here? I wonder if I should use strings or a wood-wind instrument on the melody?" The arranger should have a timing
sheet as he begins to orchestrate in order to get the mood of a
scene and know the dialogue spots. He can then arrange accordingly.

The association of melodies with certain parts of the Unit-
ed States has been established. The folk songs paint different
mental pictures of the various parts of the country where they
originated, or the parts they describe. For example, when you
think of the South, you hear a Negro spiritual or one of Stephen
Foster's folk songs.

One of Foster's songs is associated with the West because
it was the song that the pioneers sang in the days when they
were moving westward. It is a good banjo tune, lively, and one
that describes their wonderful spirit. It is "Oh, Susanna!" You
can use these songs for patterns.

Cowboy songs paint a mental picture of the West, just as
spirituals and cake-walks do of the South. They are similar in
chord construction—very simple harmonies, sometimes using no
more than three chords, the tonic, sub-dominant and dominant
seventh.

Every country has its characteristic music, such as Spanish,
Irish, Mexican (similar to Spanish), Chinese, Arabian, French,
etc.

Naturally, when you are concerned with a certain locale,
you pattern your writing after the music associated with it. You
have just studied the music in this story—the locale being Ireland, the music was Irish in character throughout.

The spiritual type, to describe the South, could be:

The harmony is simple, only two chords, the tonic and sub-dominant. This would be easy to arrange for strings. It is quartette writing, therefore, the violins would play the melody; the violas, the second line, the B's and C's; the celli, the third line, the D's and B's; and the bass the lowest line. If you wished to use one of the wood-winds on the melody (perhaps the English horn), you would replace the violins with the English horn, using the violas, celli and bass background.

A cake-walk type could be:

Notice that the harmonic construction retains that simple, folk-song flavor. The arrangement of this type of number can be done in several ways: It could feature strings, a combination of strings and wood-winds, or full orchestra. For example, a string arrangement:

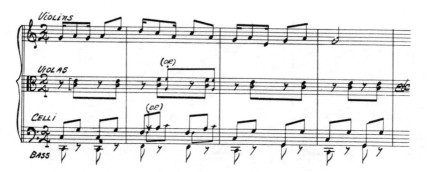

The violins play the melody; the violas play the E and C notes of the after-beat chords with double-stops; and the celli play four notes in a bar, the bass note in octaves with the bass, and the lower note (G) of the after-beat chord with the violas.

The violins can either play in unison as they are written or divisi, half of them an octave higher.

It is better to use some wood-winds in an arrangement of this type to give some support to the strings. They not only tie it together, but establish the chord construction. The following type of wood-wind background would enhance the arrangement:

If you wanted to use the wood-winds to play the melody, you could use the flute and oboe on the melody in octaves, the clarinets on the sustained harmony, and divide your strings on the after-beats, which are very important in a number like this.

For example, the following is one of wood-winds and strings:

In this example the violins are mixed with the violas on the after-beats. The celli now only play with the bass in octaves.

There are several ways you can divide the strings, depending on the required amount of volume you want. For instance, the three-note chord could be divided:

Here the first violins would only play one note, the E; the second violins, the C; and the violas, the G. This can be played lightly or with power, depending upon the amount of strings you have in the orchestra.

A mixture of double-stopped chords in the strings could be:

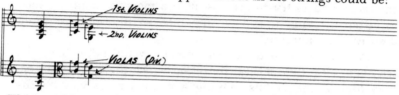

This would be a full-sounding chord and have power (another note, G, has been added).

To arrange this number for full orchestra, the key should be changed. The key should be one in which the brass parts are not too low, or the arrangement will sound "muddy." The key of E flat would be more brilliant and a better register for the brass.

As indicated here, all of the violins and wood-winds would play the melody in octaves. The brass, instead of playing melody, would play chord formations in a rhythmic pattern. In the fourth bar, the trumpets would imitate the melodic phrase. The brass, being written in this rhythmic pattern, would give life and a lift to the rhythm of the number. The violas and horns would play after-beats with the piano and drums. The bassoon could have a pattern, such as:

This reinforces the rhythmic pattern.

It is well to remember that a number of this type is characteristic, and to try to arrange it in a modern manner (such as re-harmonizing it and writing modern figurations) would destroy your purpose.

Another way to treat this number would be to have the trumpets play the melody, the wood-winds the melody an octave higher, the violins playing a counter-melody, with the rhythmic section playing the same as before. For example (but notice that the trombones are written in the same pattern as before to avoid a "loggy" feeling in the rhythm):

Another way to treat this number would be to add more strings to the violin line. Instead of dividing the violins, write them in unison on the upper line and write the violas on the octave below.

Still another way would be to add the celli to the violins and violas. Then the string line would be in three octaves. For example:

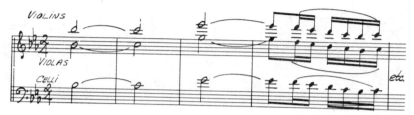

The melody should be reinforced to balance with this amount of strings. You could do this by writing the first trombone on the melody, in octaves with the first trumpet. For example:

In the analysis of folk songs we have noted that they employ simple harmonic construction. It is also interesting to note that a Western tune has two definite characteristics which label it "Western": one is the added sixth and the other is the ending. Most tunes end with a dominant seventh chord before the tonic, but the Western tune ends with a secondary seventh, or a sub-dominant chord, before the tonic. For example:

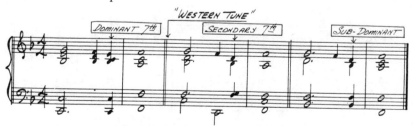

The secondary seventh or sub-dominant chord gives the tune what has been established as that "cowboy" sound.

An example of a Western or an outdoor theme is the following:

This has the sound of the Western open spaces. (Notice the sixth on the second and fourth beats of the first bar.)

There are many ways to arrange this number, and the orchestration is very important in describing the Western outdoor scene. First, the French horn, the oboe, the English horn, the clarinet and the flute are the best instruments to describe an outdoor scene. The key used in the example, E flat, is good for the French horn or English horn solo.

If the choice happened to be the French horn, it would depend upon the volume you wished the horn to play just how heavy the background should be written. If the volume would be "*mp*", the strings, reinforced with some wood-winds, would be correct for the background. This would not submerge the horn solo. For example:

If the English horn plays the melody, the strings alone would be better, omitting the wood-winds.

A note should be made here that the size of the orchestra, especially the amount of strings that you have, determines how to write for a balance. This example is written for an orchestra that does not have a full string section. For that reason, the strings are given a little support by the wood-winds.

With a full string section, this background may be too heavy for a solo instrument. It would then be good for two or more horns to play in unison on the melody.

For soft wood-wind solos, if your orchestra has a large string section, it is better to use only a part of the section for the background, written in a quartette fashion as much as possible.

Another way to treat this Western theme is to create a pastorale effect in the upper register and have the horns (in unison) and the celli on the melody in its original register. This treatment paints an outdoor picture and has the sound of the open spaces. There are several ways to write the chords in the upper instruments, which should be shakes. For example:

Any of these patterns could be used or a combination of two of them. Pattern #1 employs the sixth, but #2, #3, and #4 uses another note, F, making some of the voices move in fourths, which is better. The following is an example employing #2 and #3 patterns:

In the analysis you see that pattern #3 was written for the strings, and pattern #2 was written for the wood-winds. This will sound full and be a good background for the horns and celli.

Notice that on the third beat of the second bar the harmony changes to an A flat as in the sketch of the original; so by keeping the same formation, the notes were changed to form an A flat sixth chord.

Examining the chords as a cluster, they look like this:

For a better effect, it would be well to add the harp to the upper instruments with arpeggios, such as:

The divisi of the violins in the upper voices in the preceding sketch would depend on the number you have in the orchestra. Divide them equally on each part.

If you wanted to use the violas with the violins on the shakes, a different pattern should be used in a lower register to keep the violas in a better range, such as pattern #2.

As this type of arrangement sounds from the middle register up, the bass or any low wood-winds are tacet.

Another way to .treat this number would be to write all of the strings in unison on the melody. The key of E flat is good, but the key of E major would be a better choice for the strings. The quality would be rich and sonorous. The English horn could be added to the strings and a figuration with the other wood-winds used to give it a pastorale effect. The horns and trombones could play the harmony in the lower register, below the strings. The harp and celeste could play a chord accompaniment, employing the sixth of the chord. This treatment has a wonderful sound.

Let us look at a sketch of this nature. The harmony is changed slightly. Instead of writing a sub-dominant chord in the second half of bar 2, the secondary seventh chord is used. This chord continues throughout bar 3.

This arrangement is rich, full and picturesque, and should be used in open portions of the picture, not under dialogue.

Let us consider an oboe or a clarinet solo. The melody could be played an octave higher on either instrument, but the high B natural and C sharp are rather thin on the oboe and rather shrill on the clarinet. For these reasons a change of key would be better. The keys of C or D flat would be good for both instruments. The clarinet is good in the middle register. The following example shows a clarinet solo with a string background:

This key, G, is good for strings, especially in the upper register. This key is also good for full orchestra, employing the trumpets.

Let us look at an example (not full) in which the violins play the melody in the upper register, the wood-winds a pastorale effect, and featuring the horns on a counter-melody. The horns are important in a number like this:

The lower harmony should be strong enough to form a good foundation for the horns, wood-winds and strings in the upper voices. The third clarinet and bassoon should be added to the lower harmony in tenths. The complete wood-winds would look like this:

If you want a rich sound, add three trombones to be played softly. They could be written thus:

Another way to treat this arrangement would be to write the violas on the melody in octaves with the violins; write the celli in unison with the horns; the wood-winds would remain the same; and the trombone chords the same but marked "*mf.*" This treatment would have more power.

There are many patterns for the wood-wind section in a number such as this. You have seen two. Another good one is crossing the parts, as follows:

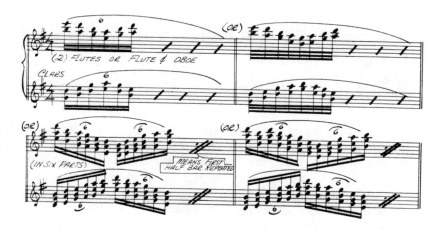

These patterns are good for either the wood-winds or the strings — violins and violas.

If you want to use the full orchestra on this number, including the trumpets, it is better to have all of the strings on the melody if you do not have a large string section; the brass playing a quasi-organ background; the wood-winds a pastorale effect, but in the upper register so that they can be heard; the horns can reinforce the melody with the strings, or play with the brass section in the organ effect, or even play a counter-melody (not the one used in the previous sketch because the brass might submerge it), something like an echo might be good.

Let us look at a sketch of the strings, horns, trumpets and trombones:

This arrangement would be more brilliant in key of Bb.

To this would be added the wood-winds on a pastorale effect in the upper register, the low wood-winds with the trombones, the bass, the harp and the percussion. A good effect would be a cymbal on the third beat of the first bar.

After studying the preceding sketches, you can see that it is an asset to know the orchestra when writing a score. There are many ways to arrange a scene, and the composer should think in terms of the orchestra when writing for mood.

Almost anything can be described in music, especially with the orchestra. You have heard train effects, donkey brays, chicken cackles and machine effects. For example, a train effect:

After four bars of rhythm, such as this, other elements could be added, like a horn figuration. For example:

This could be developed into a longer phrase with wood-winds added in octaves with the horns.

A machine effect could be written:

The monotony of the rhythm soon sounds mechanical. The horns could be developed into a longer theme.

A donkey bray can be imitated in this manner:

A chicken cackle could be imitated in this manner:

A factory or a foundry could be imitated in this manner:

These chords are built on fourths. The orchestration is important. The violins and violas can be added to the horn and trombone chords or written on a theme based upon this chord construction. The percussion can play the steel plate, tympani and cymbals.

MORE ABOUT THEMES

It is possible to create one theme and by variations or harmonic changes to construct several different moods from that one.

As an example, we will analyze a score I wrote. The main story line was of a patriotic nature. It was a modern American story with sabotage as the menace.

The principal theme was of the noble character and had a slightly patriotic sound:

My first thought was to create it in a key in which the register would be good for a string unison or a horn solo. The key of D was good for both. The melodic line and the harmonic construction were suitable for a noble, patriotic march. This could be done with a four-beat rhythm.

As a string number, without rhythm, it was just right, and

it was also good for a horn solo with string accompaniment.

Then I took the melodic line and re-harmonized it for a menace theme:

There are two alterations in the melody in bar 1 — instead of C sharp, the C is natural, and instead of E natural, the E is flat.

This could be orchestrated in several ways — powerfully or menacingly without being loud. For instance, a soft menace:

The string tremolo could stop with the horns on the fourth beat of the third bar. The wood-winds would continue the descending scale over the bass notes.

For power you could use the horns open, add the violins to the horns, and add trombones on the harmony.

Next I took the principal theme and constructed a love theme. With a few melodic alterations and harmonic changes, I wrote the following:

Two pick-up notes have been added. The first bar melodic line is the same as the original, but with a harmonic change. Instead of starting with the tonic chord the harmony has been changed to a secondary seventh chord.

As an agitato, I did the following:

Here the agitato is created by the strings and tympani. At the third bar the wood-winds enter with the principal theme, answered by the horns at bar 5.

To describe a fight scene, a good device is to write a piece of music that has off-beat accents. As the fists fly around, the orchestra is hitting uneven rhythms, adding excitement to the fight. These scenes can be done to click track, as was done in "THE IRISHMAN" score, catching the action as it happens, but in a dramatic fight a free piece of music creates the excitement without being too "Mickey Mouse."

For example, a dramatic fight (free, not to click track):

Notice the off-beat brass in bars 5 and 6.

The use of dissonant chords is good to describe shock or pain. As an example:

A B flat major and a D major are struck together. This chord could be played by the trumpets and trombones, muted or open, or by the trumpets and horns, muted or open, or with the strings tremolo reinforced with the wood-winds and horns, or by all of the instruments combined. Another example follows:

In balancing this chord the strings and wood-winds could be divided on the four top notes (the strings tremolo). The

three trumpets could play the C sharp, B, and G, with two horns
or one trombone on the E.

The seconds in the trumpets, C sharp and B, would be
more effective than if the three trumpets were divided on the
three lower notes, B, G, and E.

Another example would be:

This chord would really screech because of the double
minor seconds. The strings and the wood-winds could play this
(with string tremolo). To give it impact, the piano could strike
the chord with force on the down-beat.

The piano is very effective when used as a percussion
instrument. As an example of this, the following could be used
to describe tragedy. In it the piano has an important part:

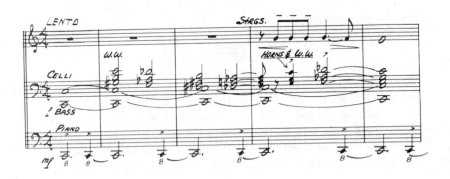

The piano is also effective playing low chords. As an
example of this, note the following illustration which might
be used for a fog scene or perhaps a harbor with a feeling of
mystery or suspense:

The alto flute creates a lonesome sound, while the low chords in the strings and the piano and the high tremolo in the violins create a feeling of mystery.

Another good effect with the piano is shown in the following example. Here it plays trills, and in this subdued number, the piano gives it a sort of diffused sound.

The piano, when used in a large orchestra, should be considered a percussion instrument, to reinforce chords, especially those in the lower register or to add impact to a dramatic chord. For instance, a low, dramatic chord played by the trombones, horns and low wood-winds:

In the last two bars the piano doubling the bass reinforces the percussion effect of the march tempo. The right hand does not double the horns and trombones.

In the score of "THE IRISHMAN" almost every problem of writing a score was encountered except one. That is a montage. A montage is a trick-shot process which is used for several different purposes.

The most common one is a newspaper montage which tells some part of the story in headlines, such as "Gray Convicted"— etc. These can be dramatic, neutral, and comedy. The music should be of the same character as the montage.

Another type is one showing a lapse of time. In other words, a series of shots show what the characters in the story are doing during that lapse of time. This is a series of fast dissolves or they can also superimpose the shots. In this type the music should also describe the action and the mood of the shots.

The montage is generally silent (no dialogue), and therefore, the music is very important to help in the story progression.

There is another type, however, in which there may be a series of shots with dialogue. The following is an example of one of these. There is a call to arms — a sort of rally — showing different men in different locales giving speeches to groups of men. You will notice chords, accented on each cut, and a "subito *p*" with a dramatic effect sustained under the short speeches. The "*ff*" chords, played as the scenes change, are very effective.

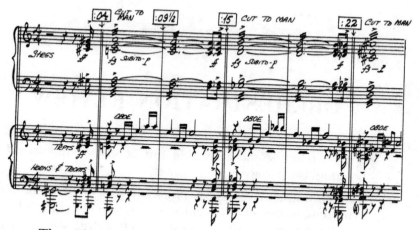

These chords punctuate each cut in the picture. The string tremolo and the oboe sustain the drama under the dialogue.

After analyzing many thematic ideas and the orchestrations it may be helpful to some students to review orchestration.

CHAPTER FOUR

ORCHESTRATION REVIEW

O RCHESTRATION and arranging can be classed in two different categories:

1. Orchestrating is a process whereby the orchestrator distributes, in the correct balance, a composition in sketch form to the different instruments in the orchestra.

2. Arranging is a process whereby the arranger creates the many embellishments, harmonizations, modulations, counter melodies, introductions, and endings in the arrangement he makes of a melody. He may do this from a simple piano part, or from a lead sheet of the melody.

In the studios today there are these two classifications because there is so much music that is written in sketch form such as the underscore. The composer has a complete composition which is turned over to the orchestrator. If he turns over a melodic line with some indicated harmonies, that would come under the heading of arranging. The arranger has to create a composition out of it.

The Musician's Union has a scale price for these two catagories.

There are many types of music used in pictures. To be versatile is an asset.

There is a heavy dramatic music that requires a deft hand in orchestrating, one who knows the symphony orchestra; musical comedy types that require a man who knows the popular style and how to write for a large orchestra; jazz music types that require a man who can write in that style. If you can do all three, you are more in demand.

216

As a rule, the real jazz is written by those who make that a specialty.

There have been many dance band arrangers who have been successful in all three of these types of music as arrangers, and later composers, of underscoring music.

STRING WRITING

The obstacle that seems to bother most dance band arrangers in the motion picture field is the string section. That is understandable because of the lack of practice and experience with a good string section that the jazz element has not developed.

The difference between writing for a symphony orchestra and a studio or radio orchestra, is the amount of strings that you have to write for.

In a symphony you may have 16 first violins (or more), 14 second violins (or more), 12 violas (or more), 8 celli (or more), and 6 basses (or more).

In symphonic writing the treatment is more quartette writing, so there is a natural balance of strings when four note chords or four moving parts are distributed.

For example a four note chord:

Even though there are five notes in these chords the basic chord is one of four notes. One of the notes is doubled in octaves.

An example of quartette writing with the strings in a natural balance is the following:

The division of this is very simple. The first violins would play the top line, the second violins the second line, the violas the third line, the celli the fourth line, and the bass in octaves with the celli.

It is possible to write a wider spread chord by dividing the strings but the power is weakened somewhat because there are fewer instruments on each note. For example:

You will notice it is possible to divide the basses also. (See third and fourth bars).

By having so many divisis the basses would overpower the weakened upper voices.

When writing for strings it is well to remember the ratio of balance. Owing to their respective sizes the ratio is 2 violins (in unison) to 1 viola, 2 violas (in unison) to 1 cello and 2 celli (in unison) to 1 bass.

The basic quartette of strings is composed of 2 violins, 1 viola and 1 cello. Quartette playing is somewhat different than symphony playing because the four players are in close contact with each other, listening to one another, and balancing their volume to a certain extent.

In orchestra playing, the string balance should be written into the score with the ratio kept in mind when dividing the strings.

As studio or radio orchestras do not use as many strings

as the symphony orchestra the string sections are planned in the above ratio.

For dramatic music it is good to have plenty of low strings. Some writers, orchestrators and arrangers may have their own pet divisi, therefore the amount may vary.

Some standard string sections in the studios may have 16 violins, 6 violas, 4 celli and 2 basses; others 12 violins, 3 or 4 violas, 3 or 4 celli and 1 or 2 basses; 10 violins, 3 or 4 violas, 2 celli and 1 bass; 8 violins, 2 or 3 violas, 2 celli and 1 bass.

They may have 3 basses in a large orchestra but one doubles tuba and plays with the brass section most of the time.

As a division of strings weakens the volume, it is better to reinforce (especially the lower ones) with the woodwinds. The middle register can be reinforced also without destroying the string quality.

The most effective arrangement is the violins divisi in octaves and the harmony in the lower strings.

In the student's summary you have seen several treatments of the strings. However for the students who have not had much experience, we will analyze the string balance for the orchestra, the distribution of a chord, and divisi of small and standard orchestras.

For example, a four note chord would be written:

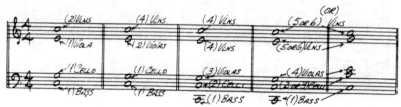

With a section as small as 2 violins, 1 viola, 1 cello and bass, a wide-spread chord could be written:

The violins, viola, and cello can be written as a unit. This divisi would be good if the strings were augmented in ratio. For example:

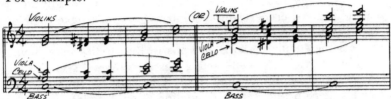

In the first two bars, the voicing is in close harmony. In bars three and four, the voicing is open harmony. This division would be more effective by adding more strings. For instance, if you have 12 violins, 3 violas, 2 celli, and 1 bass, the violins would be divided 6 and 6 on the two top notes, and the violas and celli unison on the notes that are written for them in the example.

If you have sufficient strings, it is possible to write the violins divisi in the upper register while the violas, celli, and bass play the chord in the lower register.

The following examples show the violins divisi in octaves — in 3 parts, and in 4 parts. (Don't write in 4 parts unless you have sufficient violins.)

These chords are wide-spread, and you will notice that there is a very large gap between the violins in the upper register and the low strings. There is nothing in the middle register. This can be corrected in three ways: Raise the harmony parts an octave which will sound weaker; or add wood-winds. The wood-winds could be written in the middle register; or divide your lower strings and reinforce them with wood-winds.

For example:

The divisi of strings in the first two bars (low violas and celli) will have more power than in the last two because of the divisi in the violas and celli. (The oboe could play the melody with the lower violins.) The effect in the last two bars would have a rich string sound however, and be good for "*p*" or "*mp*" passages.

The violin distribution in a divisi depends upon the amount you have to write for. For instance: If you have 4 violins to divide on a 3 note chord, you would put 2 on the top note, (the melody) and 1 on each of the harmony notes. For 4 parts, 1 on each note.

With 8 violins, (a bad divisi for a 3 note chord) 4 on the top note (the melody) and 2 on each harmony note. For 4 parts, 2 on each note.

With 10 violins, 4 on the top note, (the melody) and 3 on each harmony note. For 4 parts, (an awkward divisi) 3 on the top note, (the melody) 2 on each harmony note, and 3 on the melody an octave below the first line.

With 12 violins, 4 on each note. For 4 parts, 3 on each note.

With 16 violins, 6 on the top note, (the melody) and 5 on each harmony note. For 4 parts, 4 on each note.

Whenever you have a number of violins that can not be divided by three, write the odd ones on the top, or melody line, on a 3 note chord.

POPULAR MUSIC

In popular music, the style of writing for strings has changed. Instead of the viola being confined to after beats, and the cello doubling the bass, or with a counter melody, they are written with the violins as a section. The violins are not divided into first and second violins, but are used as a whole.

In the old days, the string section was treated as a symphony orchestra. The second violins and violas were written as a rhythm section, which is correct in a concert number with a very large string section for a march, waltz, or any light number requiring after beats. However, in modern dance music, the piano, drums, bass, and guitar take care of the rhythm. Therefore, the strings are written as a section which facilitates more effective and interesting results.

The following illustrates the old-fashioned style of a popular type of melody:

In an orchestra that has a rhythm section, this is a waste of strings. It sounds thin. It isn't rhythmic. The after beats will never be as rhythmic as the four beats of the guitar and drums, with the piano playing the after beats.

Let's try some different treatments. First, the counter melody could be utilized by writing it in unison for the strings, while the melody is being played in another section. For instance, saxophones:

Strings in unison on a counter melody, or the melody, have a wonderful sound.

Second, we will have the strings alone:

Here violins are divided on the two top notes, the violas unison on the third note, and the celli, the melody an octave lower than the violins. The only instance the celli did not play the melody is in the fourth bar. By resolving to the B, we have the four notes of the G ninth chord.

Another way; raise the phrase an octave. (All parts.)

And another way; leave it in the lower register and write in mostly four part harmony.

This could all be in four part harmony. But by leaving the sixth out of the first chord and the fourth beat, the sound improves when the celli move from the G to the A in the diminished chord on the third beat, and back to the melody note G on the fourth beat.

Another way would be to raise the melody an octave and
write it in open harmony:

A string section of twelve violins, four violas and two celli
offers an opportunity for a rich divisi such as the following:

This could be divided — three violins on each top four
notes — the violas divided on the F# and D, and two celli on
the lower note (melody). Here the melody is doubled in three
octaves with the inter-harmonies.

This would sound even more effective if the lower harmonies were reinforced with wood-winds. It would still retain
its string color. The wood-winds could be:

The fourth note, or the melody, can also be added an
octave lower. To add the wood-winds in the upper register de-
tracts from the string color.

RHYTHM NUMBERS

As a rule, a large orchestra with a large string section
is not rhythmic, but rather "loggy". Therefore, the strings
should be used sparingly. Refrain from writing rhythmic patterns in jazz tunes. If the number has a melodic release, the
strings are good for color. They are effective on a bass pattern, or a short phrase in unison at times, such as:

SWEET NUMBERS AND VOCALS

In melodic or sweet numbers the strings can have the important parts, such as melody, counter melodies, or phrases you would write for the saxophones or wood-winds, written in the balances you have just seen.

In vocal arrangements, the strings can be very important. For better results, the melody should be omitted and the instruments written only as a background to the melody of the singer. This gives the singer more freedom to do his phrasing without any interference from the orchestra.

If a part of the number is done out of rhythm, (rubato) different types of effects can be used. The following example illustrates a chord sustained under the voice. A movement or a "fill-in" occurs at the end of the singer's phrase:

With this accompaniment, the singer has freedom to phrase in his own style, while the orchestra plays an interesting background.

This treatment is also good for the strings if the number is in rhythm. Instead of writing the strings in the lower register, they could be written in the upper register in a rhythmic pattern with a pizzicato bass.

Here the strings play the background in four part close harmony, the strings are richer if kept in close position. If a sixth is employed they could be written thusly:

The wood-winds are written in close harmony in this sketch instead of open as in the previous sketch. The rhythm section plays straight rhythm.

A good background for a singer is to write the violins in thirds in the upper register, with the violas and celli on the harmony. For example:

This arrangement has more movement and could be played rubato or in rhythm by adding the rhythm section and woodwinds.

DOUBLE STOPS

How to use double and triple stops often confuses the dance arranger.

Sometime ago a boy brought me an arrangement, and he had a double stop written for the violins like this:

He had never stopped to realize that both of those notes are played upon the same string, the G string.

We know that the strings of the instruments are:

    Violin—G - D - A - E.

    Viola—C - G - D - A.

    Cello—C - G - D - A.

You can see why some double stops are impossible.

In symphonic music you can get a powerful chord with the strings divided in a wide spread chord.

The following example illustrates chords with double and triple stops.

These chords could either be played arco (bowed) or pizzicato. The arco chords would lend more power and volume than pizzicato. A good example of a string chord is in the fight music in the preceding chapter.

WOOD-WINDS AND HORNS

The horns can play with either the wood-wind or the brass sections. For the best results they should be played with the wood-winds, for the blend of wood-winds and horns has a wonderful sound.

The voicing of wood-winds can be done in many ways; a close position chord to a wide-spread chord. For example, a chord voiced in different positions. By examining the position and divisi of the chords, can be seen the difference in power and brilliancy.

The chords are mellow and softer if the clarinets are written in the middle register, and brilliant if written in the upper register.

Because the flute is weak in volume in the lower register, it should be doubled with another instrument if used on the top of a triad. For example:

The flute and oboe unison, or flute and English horn unison, gives the chord a slight difference in tone color.

In sections where you have two flutes, two oboes, two clarinets, bass clar, and two bassoons, you could voice in the following manner:

When you add the horns to the wood-winds, they enhance the color and the beauty of the chord. The horns can reinforce the middle register.

For example, one flute, one oboe, two clarinets, two horns, one bass clarinet and bassoon:

Three horns are more effective because you then have a triad that can be written in close or open harmony.

Four horns can be written in unison, divided by two's, or in four parts. In four parts the top note is most generally doubled an octave below:

THE DOUBLING OF WOOD-WINDS

When doubling wood-winds on a melody or counter melody, there are several problems one may encounter: 1. The register. 2. How prominent you wish the solo to be. 3. How much background you are going to write.

The oboe tone penetrates more than the clarinet in the middle register, therefore the oboe solo will be heard with a medium amount of strings as a background, while the clarinet may be obscured.

If you have a large string section, it is possible to use one-half of the strings for the background, the second violins, first stand violas, and the first stand celli and basses.

You can double an oboe solo with the flute (in unison), which will give the solo a little more prominence and yet retain an oboe color. In fact, it takes away some of the harshness of the low tones of the oboe.

The clarinet can also be doubled with the oboe, or the flute, with good results. However, if you want the pure tone of a solo instrument, they should play alone, with the background written light enough for them to be heard.

Wood-winds are more penetrating in the upper registers, therefore the background should be written accordingly. For loud wood-wind passages the instruments can be doubled in octaves, or three octaves. The following example illustrates the registers where light, medium and heavy backgrounds should be written:

In bar (1), there is a wide-spread chord. This could be used with a medium amount of strings. The second chord, a three note chord, is good for a string background. The third chord is without any bass, and is a good background for a soft solo.

In bar (2), the same chords could be used, but with all of the strings. If you have a small amount, three wood-winds can be added.

In bar (3), the same chords can be used with all of the strings plus the horns.

If a piccolo is added, the wood-winds would then be in three octaves. A bassoon could be added on the octave below, with four octaves of wood-winds.

BRASS

A standard brass section is composed of three trumpets and three trombones.

The difference between writing for a dance band and a concert orchestra is in the voicing. In dance band music, the voicing is most generally in close harmony with added sixths:

In symphony writing the brass is utilized mostly for climaxes, chord accents, chord foundations in forte passages, and soft harmony backgrounds, they can be written in the following manner:

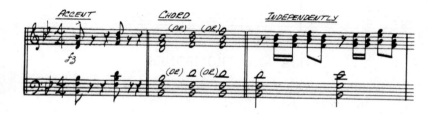

If the composition is in concerted form, the brass can also be in concerted form — the trumpet playing melody.

For example:

In the symphony, the third trombone most generally is a bass trombone. It is possible then to write a low chord such as the following:·

The low note on the tenor trombone being E, it would be impossible to play the above, but with the bass trombone, the chords are powerful.

HORNS AND TROMBONES

The horns can be written with the trombones, but two horns should be written in unison to balance with one trumpet, or one trombone:

TUBA AND TROMBONES

The tuba can be written with the trombones, and is very effective in low chords:

HARP AND CELESTE

To gain an understanding of the harp, the student should purchase an instruction book for study. He must learn the pedals, and what is most technically feasible to play for maximum results from this instrument. This being a lengthy subject, only a few hints are shown here pertaining to the treatment in the orchestration.

The most effective treatments are chords and arpeggios, depending upon the nature of the composition.

Chords on the down beats are effective on numbers that have movement. Numbers that do not have movement in the other instruments can be embellished with harp arpeggios:

The harp is also effective on glissandos for a change of key, or to lead up to an accent:

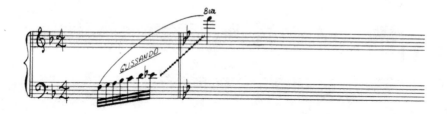

The celeste and harp can play together effectively on arpeggios or chords. A good example of chords was shown in one of the treatments of the Western theme in the Student's Summary.

FULL ORCHESTRA BALANCE

The distribution and divisi of a chord for the orchestra in proper balance depends upon the amount of instruments you have to write for, and the desired intensity of sound, or volume.

In an orchestra that does not have full sections, the distribution of the notes should vary from that of a large orchestra, to reinforce the weaker sections.

A chord can become top heavy with no bottom, or bottom heavy with no top. When using brass, the distribution should be different because of their power. They take care of the middle register when the full orchestra is playing double forte.

In some of the previous examples, (wood-winds and horns) you have seen the distribution of notes to the various wood-winds and horns. This type of distribution would be good if used with the strings only, providing you divide your strings to the best advantage, according to the amount you have. With full orchestra, including brass, the upper register is weak. Therefore, it will be a better balanced chord if you write your wood-winds in the octave above the brass. It is best to include the horns in your brass chord in the middle register. The voicing of the trombones can be two ways; open or close harmony.

The following chart shows the distribution of a chord for a medium sized orchestra, for recording:

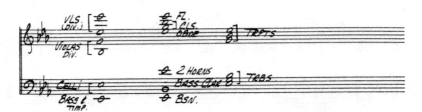

This chord will sound full, but the lows are a little weak. In analyzing the chord, you see that the brasses and horns furnish a solid middle register of two octaves. In the upper register, the volume is weakened by writing the violins divisi, (if you have a medium number). This could be strengthened by writing them in unison on the melody note, the high E flat.

The clarinets are brilliant on the B flat and G, but the brass section still overpowers them. The oboe is obliterated by the trumpet.

A balance could be obtained by marking the wood-winds and strings "*ff*" and the brass and horns "*mf*", but, to get an equal balance, double forte, the wood-winds, violins and trumpets could be written:

Here the violins play in unison on the melody, (if you have another flute, write it on the violin line, E flat) the flute and oboe are doubled on the B flat, the first and second clarinets doubled on the G, and the triad of trumpets below.

In the division of the original chord, you see the octave played by the horns and trombones is strong, but below that it weakens because there is only a bass clarinet on the B flat and the bass on the low E flat.

One way to strengthen the lower part of the chord is to divide the violas and celli lower:

Another way would be to write the trombones in open harmony. If you have a tuba, the chord is perfect:

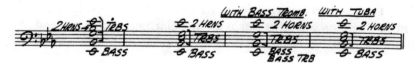

When arranging, the object is to get the maximum sound from the orchestra.

In a large orchestra of symphony size, the tone color is

improved by dividing the strings as a full chord in four or five parts within themselves; the wood-winds in the upper register, the horns with them in the middle register, the bassoons and bass clarinets in the lower register, the brass in a wide spread chord.

The doubling of the different types of instruments on the notes of the chord produce a sound which is rich in quality.

In a large orchestra, with a full violin section, the violins can be divided in octaves and still have power. The effect is better because an octave melody is more effective and the lower line violins reduce the shrillness, or edge of the high first violins. With the violins in octaves, the wood-winds furnish the inter-harmonies. For example, in a large orchestra, on a double forte passage, the distribution can be two ways in the upper register:

The above illustrates very loud passages.

For forte passages, or mezzo forte passages:

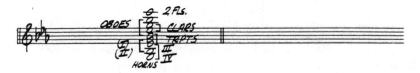

The lower register could be written in the following manner for the bassoons, bass clarinets, alto clarinet, trombones and tuba:

Obviously, there are many ways to divide a chord (depending upon the size of the orchestra) for fullness, sound and power.

As a final reminder; the student can gain knowledge by reviewing scores, and studying what has been written for each instrument for balance and color. It is helpful to follow the scores while listening to records, to ascertain how the instruments sound when written in a certain manner.

GLOSSARY

C.U. — Close up; camera very close, showing only the head.

M.S. — Medium shot; camera a medium distance away, showing head, shoulders.

M.L.S. — Medium long shot; a fairly long shot, showing from the waist up.

L.S. — Long shot; camera far away.

C.S. — Close shot; camera close to characters.

M.C.S. — Medium close shot; same as medium long shot.

M.C.U. — Medium close up; same as medium long shot.

2 S. — Two shot; same as medium shot, but two people.

M.2 S. — Medium two shot; same as medium long shot, with two people.

M.3 S. — Medium three shot; with three people.

CAMERA DOLLIES. — Camera moves on a small truck to follow characters.

CAMERA MOVES IN. — Rolls on the truck closer to the people.

CAMERA PANS. — Camera is on a stationary stand, but can swing around to follow the action.

EXTERIOR. — Out of doors.

INTERIOR. — Indoors.

UP-STAGE. — Toward the back of set.

238

O.S. — Off stage; not seen.

B.G. — Background.

F.G. — Toward the front of the set.

SPLICE. — Patching two pieces of film together.

RE-TAKE. — To shoot again.

LOOP. — A small strip of film patched together, making a loop.

OVERLAP. — Putting the ends of two films over each other.

MUSIC RELEASES. — To assign the performance rights to the studio.

MIXER. — The man who handles the dials when recording.

SYNC. — To synchronize.

PROP. — Any article used to dress the stage, or used in the picture.

FADE IN. — A scene gradually becomes visible.

FADE OUT. — A scene gradually becomes invisible.

DISSOLVE. — By overlapping the film, one scene fades out and the following one fades in. At one point both scenes are visible.

CUT TO. — An editor's cut from one scene to another.

SUPERIMPOSED. — Putting one element over the other.

INSERT. — Short scenes for story value, such as a letter, telegram or newspaper.

REVERSE SHOT. — Photographed from behind.

REVERSE ANGLE. — Photographed from behind and at an angle.

A TAKE. — Recording.

Photographs by

PETER GOWLAND
HERB CARLTON